"This is a book which tells the story of … n the
21st century. Each chapter un… illed
in the ministry of Jesus. It is an … ary'
people relate incidents and mo… od
at work as they live 'in step with t… 's-
siological reflection earthed in th… he
who are learning to be non judg… unity. Instead
they have become humble listeners … ospitality and so discover opportunities to preach and to practice grace. A great read."

Rev Dr Trevor Morrow
Former Moderator of the
Presbyterian Church in Ireland

"Ireland is a land of stories. Arguably, the greatest story ever told is about God coming among us in Jesus Christ. Throughout the story of Ireland generations of people have embraced the Christian story. The words and presence of Jesus Christ have given faith, hope and love to countless Irish people. Gloriously Ordinary is a book which tells the stories of some ordinary Irish Christians. These ordinary yet extraordinary people not only talk the talk but walk the talk in their witness for Christ. These big-hearted people tell of their faith and failures, longings and love, daring and disappointments. Ruth Garvey-Williams who has drawn the collection together is uniquely placed to frame these stories. As editor of VOX Magazine she has the pulse of the changing landscape of Irish cultures and a sense of the Christian communities which are represented in contemporary Ireland. This is an encouraging and essential read for our unpredictable times."

The Rt Rev Dr. Ferran Glenfield
Church of Ireland Bishop of
Kimore, Elphin and Ardagh

"The title says it all really… 'Gloriously Ordinary'! This is an extremely accessible journey of possibility and adventure for anyone interested in Kingdom mission in contemporary Ireland. It is packed with powerful images of ordinary people doing extraordinary things for the Lord. The interplay of theological thinking and practical insight along with great questions offers hope and possibility for anyone wondering what they can do to grow the Kingdom in their local place."

Rev John Alderdice
Director of Ministry,
Methodist Church of Ireland

"Every one of the contributors to this gripping book made a journey of discovery into their own locality and found the most unlikely mission opportunities. Things did not turn out as they had intended but, by responding to each situation as they found it, they saw the kingdom of heaven come in unexpected ways. Their experiences can open our eyes to see the possibilities that may be hiding in plain sight in our own gloriously ordinary situations."

James Reilly
Christian Churches Ireland

"Gloriously Ordinary is a refreshing look at Missions in an Irish context written by God's agents living and serving Him in different parts of our nation. It is both encouraging and challenging and for me emphasises again the need for all followers of Jesus, to still their souls, to listen carefully, to discern correctly and to obey promptly. An important part of this book are the questions at the end of each of the seven chapters under the heading 'Take Time to Ponder.' Why? If we don't pause to think through some of these questions, we are in danger of just reading another book on Missions and not letting the Holy Spirit use it to speak to us and perhaps change how we look at or do mission in our own context."

Trevor Hill
Pastor of River of Life Church, Athlone and
Team Leader of Plumbline Ireland Ministries

"This book is a small treasure for those involved in mission and ministry. Offering principles rooted in experience, story and reflection, (rather than theories or impossible standards), Ruth and her co-authors invite readers to find their own 'gloriously ordinary' place in the many-coloured picture of ministry they describe. With its 'Take Time to Ponder,' at the close of each chapter, this is a great book for ministry teams to share, pray and discuss. It will take them beyond 'what shall we do?' to a deeper conversation about how and why."

Dr Anne Francis
Spiritual Director at the Galilee
Spirituality Centre in Boyle, Roscommon

"The Church is the fullness of Him who fills all in all (Eph 1:23). In Gloriously Ordinary Ruth Garvey-Williams gathers insights and stories from various practitioners and innovators in the area of Incarnational Christianity. But this is no patchwork quilt of disparate contributors. This is a seamless robe that portrays the manifold unity and diversity of the Body of Christ in Ireland."

Nick Park
Executive Director, Evangelical Alliance Ireland

"In this engaging book, Ruth Garvey-Williams unpacks what it means to be missional in contemporary Ireland. She states, early in the book, that this is not primarily a theology of incarnational mission but a challenge for the church as to how we can root these truths in time and place. The book is enriched by the age old Irish tradition of storytelling. There are valuable contributions, from across the island, of "Gloriously Ordinary" people who have responded to the call to be and bring God's Kingdom to their communities."

Priscilla Reid
Christian Fellowship Church, Belfast

"A beautiful tapestry of timeless truth and everyday experience. Have we forgotten what it looks like for the gospel to be embedded in real time and place? Have we disbelieved the power of the gospel that is embodied by every believer in every part of their everyday world? Gloriously Ordinary takes us back to gospel basics to re-believe that a Glorious God has, does and will work through His Ordinary People in Gloriously Ordinary ways."

Donna Jennings
Evangelical Alliance Northern Ireland

"Ruth offers us a beautiful panorama of the quiet work of God's grace across this beloved island. Her honest and tender voice coupled with insights from remarkable Irish leaders, prove to be the perfect guide for not just what is, but what could be."

Brian Sanders
Founder of Underground Network

Gloriously Ordinary
Embracing Incarnational Mission in Contemporary Ireland

Requests for information should be sent via e-mail to Praxis Press. Visit www.praxispress.ie for contact information.

Paperback ISBN # 9781693807404

Some names and identifying details have been changed to protect the privacy of individuals.

Cover design by Adam Fleming
Interior design by Jonny Lindsay

Printed by Amazon

PraxisPress.ie

To Mum and Dad, with love.

EMBRACING INCARNATIONAL
MISSION IN CONTEMPORARY IRELAND

By Ruth Garvey-Williams

Together with:

William Hayes, Joe Donnelly, Chloe Hanan,
Marian Edwards, Emma Bolster Rodrigues,
Robert Holden and Andrew Garvey-Williams

Table of Contents

ACKNOWLEDGEMENTS

It was at a meeting of Praxis Press to discuss the launch of Fraser Hosford's book that the idea for *Gloriously Ordinary* was first conceived. We wanted to share the story of mission in contemporary Ireland through the eyes of those who live and breathe an outward focus.

My thanks to Simon Kilpatrick whose insightful questions over cups of coffee challenged me to go beyond the narrative and unpack the deeper questions.

To my co-authors William Hayes, Chloe Hanan, Marian Edwards, Emma Bolster Rodrigues, Joe Donnelly and Robert Holden. This wordsmith is lost for words to express the depth of my respect, admiration and gratitude for the work you do all year round, and for your partnership in writing and shaping this book.

My sincere and heartfelt thanks to my editors who each brought such insight in honing our manuscript from a rough first draft to the finished book. To Brian Sanders for the big picture understanding that brought clarity and cohesion. To Patrick Mitchell for such thoughtful and constructive critical analysis. And to Fraser Hosford for walking with me each step of the way with unswerving encouragement and careful, detailed feedback.

Thank you to Alisa Rehn and the team of proofreaders, to Adam Fleming for the cover design and to Jonny Lindsay, my colleague and my friend, for the interior design.

To our prayer group in Buncrana; you have truly been a safe haven for us as we journey together in this faith adventure.

To my beautiful daughters, Susie and Bethany. I am in awe of your strength, your resilience and your courage. Thank you for your loving encouragement.

And to Andrew. We have walked this road side by side; sometimes weeping, often wrestling and always learning. There is a limp in our step these days but we are in for the long haul and I would not have it any other way. My love always.

Introduction

"But we have this treasure in jars of clay..." 2 Corinthians 4:7

My first attempt was a complete disaster.

Learning to bake sourdough bread during the Covid-19 pandemic seemed like such a good idea. If Facebook was anything to go by, people all over Ireland were producing artisan loaves of home-baked bread by the baker's dozen, despite the flour shortage.

Step-by-step blogs and YouTube videos suggested the whole process was easy. I imagine that definition was intended for those with plenty of time on their hands rather than someone trying to juggle work deadlines with coordinating local Covid-19 community responses.

However, I eventually did achieve an active sourdough starter and set out to make my first loaf with some degree of excitement. That initial enthusiasm waned when I realised the sheer amount of time required. Having failed to read the instructions properly, I ended up with an enormous ball of dough that stuck to the pan during baking - leaving most of the crust behind when I tried to serve it out. The finished result resembled a giant sponge.

At that point, I was close to giving up but I continued to feed my 'pet' (the way my family described my precious sourdough starter) and eventually plucked up the courage to try again. With plenty of patience (and a rare-for-me attention to detail), I lifted the finished loaf out of the oven and paraded around the kitchen with pride. An article in the Irish Times for Real Bread Week had described sourdough as "even better than sliced bread."[1] I have to agree. Nothing could compare to the delicious taste and texture of that fresh home-baked bread.

The French have a term *pain ordinaire,* which literally translates as 'ordinary bread' but might be better described as daily bread. If our daily bread is ordinary, then sourdough is gloriously ordinary.

Good things rarely come in instant-mix packages and, more often than not, one-size-fits-all does not fit. Fast food may be quick and convenient but it can never compare with the taste and nutritional value of fresh ingredients and a beautiful home-cooked meal. So why is it that when it comes to mission, we have a tendency to look for formulas, quick fixes and off-the-shelf packages? We can be tempted to import 'successful' church growth models or evangelism programmes from the UK, US or Australia despite the significant difference in culture and context. Books line our shelves or fill our Kindles but we rarely see Irish authors or hear stories that speak the language of our heart.

Mission in Contemporary Ireland

In *Down With This Sort of Thing,* Fraser Hosford described the seismic shifts that have taken place in Irish culture over recent decades and took a closer look at how the gospel is good news for contemporary Ireland. He grappled with the realities of our culture with refreshing honesty that also engaged painful truths about the church. Rejecting both rose-tinted nostalgia and bleak pessimism, *Down With This Sort of Thing* left us with an invitation to approach mission with a renewed commitment, a fresh understanding of our context and a clearer vision of how the Kingdom of Heaven addresses the deepest heart cries of our land and our people.

For centuries, missionaries from this island of saints and scholars have travelled around the world. This was the traditional understanding of mission (going overseas) and many new Irish have come here expressing gratitude for the work of those Irish missionaries both in bringing the gospel and in setting up vital services such as schools and hospitals in response to local needs. With the decline of Christendom throughout Europe theologians such as Karl Barth, Karl Hartenstein and Georg Vicedom articulated a new understanding of mission - *Missio Dei* (God's mission).[2]

Chris Wright describes the Bible's "grand narrative" - the overarching theme of God's work to restore all that was broken in the fall and to establish His Kingdom of righteousness, justice and peace.[3] This is the glorious reality of redemption. Life in all its fullness, the *shalom* of flourishing communities and the renewal of all creation is made possible by God's initiative in Jesus.[4] At its heart, it is about relationship. As Paul says, "All this is from God who reconciled us to Himself through Christ..."[5]

But remarkably, throughout scripture, we see Him choosing ordinary people and sending them out as His ambassadors. Abraham and Sarah are commissioned with the promise, "All peoples on earth will be blessed through you."[6]

Jesus sends out His disciples, "As the Father sent me..."[7] He gives us the ministry of reconciliation and invites us to participate in His work of reconciling the world to Himself.[8] Samuel Escobar explains, "Here we have not only a mandate for mission but also a model of mission style in obedience to the loving design of the Father, patterned by the example of Jesus Christ and driven by the power of the Holy Spirit."[9]

Missio Dei invites us to see mission as the central calling for all believers, not as a sideline for a select few or an optional add-on to the core activities of the church. God chooses His people to participate in His purposes in the world and to join Him in His missional activity. Samuel Escobar goes further, "The church exists for mission and ... a church that is only inwards looking is not truly the church."[10]

In *Worship and Mission After Christendom* Alan and Eleanor Kreider describe an integrated approach. "... evangelism is as necessary as ever—God still invites people to be at peace with the God of love. But the God of love is also the God of mission. And God's mission is broader than evangelism. There are other areas—for example, reconciling between estranged enemies, restoring justice, building community, caring for the earth..."[11]

While there is a caution here - Stephen Neill warns, "If everything is mission, nothing is mission,"[12] when we explore mission in contemporary Ireland from our own experiences, it is with this broader understanding of *Missio Dei*. It is not a choice between word (the gospel of Jesus Christ) and deed (the outworking of God's kingdom) but an integration of word and deed in harmony with one another and empowered by the Holy Spirit.

But what does this mean for faith communities and Jesus-followers as we look out over our beloved island, with all its beauty and brokenness, its diversity and dysfunction? To be practical for a moment, it is all very well to discuss theology, missiology and contextualisation but what does it look like in practice for us as individuals and churches to be good news and to present the good news of Jesus in Ireland?

In over a decade as editor of VOX magazine, I have had unique opportunities to travel to every county in Ireland. For the annual Finding Faith Tour, I take a week out to drive around the country and visit as many different places as possible. On this epic road trip, I have had the privilege of meeting individuals, church leaders and ministry leaders from the widest possible spectrum of the body of Christ. And as I have travelled, I have seen mission in action across so many different denominations, churches and faith communities. I have met what my dad would describe as "the blokes what do it" (blokes here being an encompassing term that includes both men and women).

This book has been born out of those encounters and subsequent conversations, visits, phone calls and interviews woven together with careful reflection and one or two meltdowns (on my part). It is not and was never intended to be a biblical and theological analysis of mission (you might consider reading books by the authors previously mentioned including Chris Wright's *The Five Marks of Mission*[13]) but rather this is a collection of the stories, experiences, learning and reflections of people living and ministering in different parts of Ireland.

Our specific context, circumstances, backgrounds, individual skills and relationships vary. But we have recognised common attitudes or postures that shape our ministries. What emerged, and has come into even clearer focus in the process of writing, are six principles that underpin and inform the approaches we have embraced. These have grown at grassroots, in response to the realities of contemporary culture and our local contexts. The principles are interlinked and often overlapping but they represent so much of our shared learning both as individuals and in our faith communities.

This is not to say that these principles are the key to mission in Ireland but rather to invite you to enter into the conversation, to reflect on whether and how these principles might apply in your context and to consider what you would add.

In the following chapters, I introduce each theme (helped as always by my husband Andrew) and my co-authors contribute reflections and stories from their own context. I also include other stories from around Ireland and share examples from our own experience. Concluding each chapter, Andrew and I ask what it means for us to embrace these principles and invite you to think more deeply about your own context and response.

Who Are We?

William Hayes is originally from Monkstown in County Antrim and now lives in Tullamore, County Offaly where he has been the minister of Tullamore and Mountmellick Presbyterian Churches for the last 17 years. He is married to Rhona and they have two children, James and Isobel.

Marian Edwards and Emma Bolster Rodrigues are Church Army Evangelists based in the Centre of Mission in Ballina, County Mayo, which was established as a partnership between Church Army, the Church of Ireland Diocese of Tuam, Killala and Achonry and Ballina Churches Together (the Church of Ireland, Roman Catholic, Presbyterian and Methodist churches in Ballina). Church Army is a mission-focused community of lay people founded in England but with Centres of Mission in Ballina, Belfast and Sligo. The Church Army vision is for everyone everywhere to encounter God's love and be empowered to transform their communities through faith shared in words and action.

Emma began the work in Ballina in 2016 as Lead Evangelist. Born in Cork, she served with YWAM, before studying Applied Theology at Moorlands College. Emma is married to Robson Rodrigues, a Baptist minister from Brazil and they have two children. In 2018, Marian Edwards was also appointed as a Pioneer Evangelist. Before moving to Mayo, Marian had lived in Sligo and she had a wide experience of outreach, evangelism and youth and children's ministry alongside the Methodist Church and the Church of Ireland.

Chloe Hanan is a Dublin/Wicklow native and is the National Campus Director with Agape. The Agape team work in collaboration with other groups to make Jesus known in Ireland. On campus, they are equipping students to navigate the complexities of student life and to live missionally in their student years. Chloe has been involved with various ministries since a young age and is passionate about seeing spiritual transformation in Irish lives.

Born and reared in Ringsend in Dublin's Docklands, **Joe Donnelly** along with his wife Sharon and their team have pioneered several 'hope-shaped' outreach initiatives at The Anchorage Project operating from The Ringsend Mission Hall. The Donnellys' work includes operating children's facilities, a community café and garden centre and an initiative for serving the needs of some of the poorest communities around the world. More recently, Joe completed a Masters in Applied Theology at the Irish Bible Institute.

After first visiting Ireland on student mission teams in the 1980s, **Robert Holden** came to Arklow from the UK in 1996 along with his wife Helen and two children. They were part of establishing Bridge Christian Community in 2000. As well as leading the church, in that time he has worked in printing, manufacturing and teaching, and he currently co-directs a theatre school. Robert also serves as part of the core team of Plumbline Ministries Ireland and the executive of Irish Mission Agencies Partnership.

And the **Garvey-Williams**? I am a writer and Andrew is an artist. Thirty years ago, we joined the mission agency Operation Mobilisation (OM) in the UK where we organised citywide missions, pioneered creative ministry and taught in the Evangelism Training Centre. I also served with OM's International Communications Team. We joined OM Ireland in January 2005 serving for seven years in Donegal and around Ireland before moving into independent ministry. My colleague Jonny Lindsay and I launched VOX magazine in 2009 (with the support of OM Ireland and the Evangelical Alliance of Ireland). In Buncrana, County Donegal we lead a small multi-cultural inter-denominational prayer group and Bible study, which usually meets in our home. We work in partnership with the local Catholic Church and the Church of Ireland for projects at Christmas and Easter and most recently ran a joint Alpha Course in the local community centre.

Gloriously Ordinary

My co-authors, like Andrew and me, are marathon runners in Christian ministry; we are in it for the long haul. All of us are gloriously ordinary. We have this "treasure in jars of clay" and seek to live out the gospel in all of life.[14] We represent a wide range of different denominational and church backgrounds and we are deeply embedded in our different contexts. Some are clergy or pastors; others have a broader ministry. Our methods, focus and styles vary but each one is seeking to follow Jesus and to see His kingdom come and His will be done in Ireland as it is in heaven. We all minister individually but also together with members of our own faith communities and in collaboration with other churches and groups.

As I write, the tremors of recent years have been eclipsed by a tsunami of change brought about by a global pandemic. With routines overturned and careful plans hastily shelved, we scrambled to adjust in work, family life and in our church communities. We have learnt a whole new vocabulary, adapted to new technologies and tried out new skills, with varying degrees of competence. The constant, unchangeable truth of the gospel is a person - *Jesus Christ, the same, yesterday, today and forever.* But as we have learnt, everything else is subject to change, even things we may have once considered rock solid.

It has seemed somehow appropriate to be writing at such a time. We have all been forced to reflect, to adapt and change, to ask tough questions and to learn new ways of doing things but, for us, this process has reinforced the principles we identify here. We would love you to journey with us as we unpack what it means for us to embrace incarnational mission in contemporary Ireland and to consider what it might mean for you as an individual or in your parish, church or faith community.

The danger would be to focus on our successes when so much of the deep learning has happened in our failures. We often discover things the hard way, more like a fly-on-the-wall documentary rather than a highlight reel. This is not the end of our stories but it is a glimpse behind-the-scenes. The journey continues as we follow the Lord of the Harvest who also walks and works beside us as we go into this beautiful corner of the world.

CHAPTER ONE

Presence

"The Word became flesh and made His dwelling among us." John 1:14

Molten lava or polished glass, storm tossed or gently lapping, this mysterious stretch of water seems to have as many moods as there are hours in a day. Lough Swilly is a glacial fjord that lies between the Inishowen Peninsula and the Fanad Peninsula in County Donegal. This is the view I see from my living room window every morning. In Irish, *Loch Súilí* means 'Lake of Eyes' but it is often called the Lake of Shadows, a name that seems to capture the essence of this ever-changing sea lough. You may well experience all four seasons in one day in Inishowen but somehow the wildly changeable weather suits this place and adds to its unspoilt beauty.

Buncrana is steeped in history - stories of voyages and shipwrecks, of triumphs and tragedies. Here were loves and losses, fierce battles and stinging betrayals, the ballads of high kings and lofty lords intertwined with the humble and wholesome songs of home. Even the stones have a story to tell, when we take the time to listen. Every now and again, we stumble on treasures of the past, mass rocks, holy wells and stone crosses that are overgrown but still poignant with the scars of age.

But it is not just the scenery that takes my breath away in our beautiful corner of the world - it is the people. This may not be the place I was born but this beloved community has become our home.[1] Shaped as it has been by pain and tragedy, division and disadvantage, Buncrana will always have my heart.

I am not a dancer. In fact, you do not want to see me attempt anything approaching creative movement these days, even though I did train as a mime artist in my much younger days in ministry. That said, there were two memorable occasions when I was ready to break into jigs and reels, albeit internally.

At one time, we were sitting in the town's Indian restaurant with the volunteers from our local suicide prevention charity. A new volunteer asked that dreaded question "Where are you from?" It is usually accompanied by the much-hated phrase, "You are not from around here are you?" But before we could answer, a friend piped up, "Oh, Andrew and Ruth are more Buncrana than Buncrana."

The second occasion for celebration was a headline in our local newspaper when I had the privilege of heading out to Romania on a Team Hope shoebox distribution - "Buncrana Woman Brings Smiles of Joy." Those were beautiful, 'jigs and reels' moments of acceptance. It was as if the town was saying, "You are one of us."

One of Us

The Incarnation is one of the most profound and important doctrines of Christianity - God became one of us. Jesus moved into our neighbourhood. Or as songwriter Graham Kendrick put it, "He walked where I walked, He stood where I stand, He felt what I feel, He understands."[2] The writer to the Hebrews explains it this way, "For we do not have a high priest who is unable to feel sympathy for our weaknesses, but we have one who has been tempted in every way, just as we are – yet He did not sin."[3]

For me, *Immanuel* (meaning 'God with us') is so much more than a lovely name to sing about at Christmas: it is an earth-shattering truth.[4] Motivated by self-giving love, the Creator of the Universe is present in the mess and madness of our mundane reality. This is powerful stuff.

The Kingdom of Heaven was no longer a distant concept, an inspirational ideology or even a vague future hope. It was present and tangible on the shores of Lake Galilee, on a grassy hillside outside of Capernaum or walking through Jerusalem's dusty streets. Suddenly, the wedding guests could taste it, and it was spectacular, a bulk order of the finest vintage. The leper could feel again, his psychological and emotional restoration as important as the healing of his numb, dead skin. The blind man could see the face of God. The deaf man could hear His voice. And the grieving mother received her son back from the dead.

It even had its own distinctive aromas; delicious fried fish cooked over an open fire, the sweet fragrance of expensive perfume and the earthy smell of sweat after a long day's walk.

Jesus lived out and embodied the message He came to teach. He not only announced the coming of the Kingdom of God but He showed us what it looked like. He lived the up-side-down truths of the Beatitudes and revealed God's heart for those the world is so quick to reject - the poor, the oppressed, the outcast and the "sinner."

All this caused huge problems for the religious elite of the time. The kingdom Jesus announced and demonstrated did not look the way they thought God's kingdom should look. They wanted to contain it, manipulate it and determine who deserved it.

The subtitle of this book talks about embracing 'incarnational mission' but what is that? It begins, as with Jesus' incarnation, with moving into the neighbourhood (whether literally or figuratively) and becoming present in our communities.

For me, this is summed up in Paul's letter to the Thessalonians, "Because we loved you so much, we were delighted to share with you not only the gospel of God but our lives as well."[5] Embracing incarnational mission means that as followers of Jesus, we will not seek to shout good news from a distance. Motivated by love, we will draw near and embody the message we teach.

This is costly stuff. Just as it cost everything for Jesus to become one of us, so it will cost us if we truly seek to be present with our neighbours, friends and colleagues and to make the Kingdom of God visible. It is a journey Andrew and I began somewhat heedlessly but that has become more intentional, the more we have come to know and love our community. I may have been born English but now I bleed gold and green for Donegal. I am all in.

Let us look more closely at what this principle of presence has meant for William in County Offaly and Marian and Emma in County Mayo.

• • •

Incarnate

Tullamore

By William Hayes

There are few of us who take great pleasure or delight in our bodies. Whether thinking of how we look or our broken parts, we all love to have a good gripe. This is hardly surprising in a world where every celebrity on the front covers of magazines has had his or her shape redrawn and blemishes removed with Photoshop.

This dissatisfaction even made its way into our everyday communications in the Covid-19 lockdown. My conferencing software offered me the option to 'touch up' my appearance. When I go out on pastoral visits, I am often presented with a list of people's ailments and the various things (sometimes in too much detail) that are going wrong in their body. If our bodies are so problematic, so awkward, so embarrassing and so prone to failure then it seems strange that at the heart of Christian faith is the idea that God, who is perfect, all sufficient and all-powerful, would choose to become flesh and make His dwelling among us.

When the Bible speaks about this, it uses language that speaks of both incarnation and relationship. John introduces us to Jesus at the start of his gospel as the Word of God who is God Himself and in relationship with God.[6] John folds together ideas from the book of Genesis, Jewish wisdom literature and Greek philosophy to show us the divine nature of Jesus. The Word is with God. The Word is God. He was in an unbroken relationship with God throughout all eternity.

In our English translations we use the static word 'with' to describe Jesus' relationship to the Father. Yet in the original Greek, the word carries much more of a sense of movement. The word *πρὸς (pros)* means towards, going to, aiming for and carries a sense of dynamic movement. The eternal direction of Jesus is towards the Father.

John goes on to say, "The Word became flesh and made His dwelling among us."[7] In doing so Jesus seeks to bring us into relationship with the Father. For our sake, He becomes a full part of the human community with all of our bodily problems and physical weaknesses.

Incarnation is all about taking on limitations. The pre-incarnate Word of God created everything in the universe in His constant journey of relationship with the Father. The incarnate Son of God becomes tired and thirsty on a relatively short journey through Samaria. Incarnation involves physical and geographical limitations. Charles Wesley sums up this idea poetically in his hymn, *Let Heaven and Earth Combine*. He speaks of Christ as, "Our God contracted to a span. Incomprehensibly made Man."[8] It is an idea both comical and miraculously wonderful.

What height is the God of the universe? About five foot seven inches, if the archaeologists are right about average heights in the Roman Empire. And so Jesus is confined and bound, like the rest of us, to the physical limits of His body. He is also geographically constrained. It is strange to think that Jesus' entire ministry took place in an area a third of the size of Ireland and (although estimates vary) in a population no greater than that of the greater Dublin area.

In the first century, the Roman Empire and its geopolitical rival Persia offered the possibility of fame and of the ability to reach and speak to a sizable percentage of the world population. Jesus, in both the tempting in the wilderness and in His later ministry, chose obscurity.

So if incarnation involves the choice to be limited, what does that mean for incarnational mission? Many of our mission strategies as churches or in our own personal outreach and evangelism, involve trying to bypass or remove our personal and corporate limitations in order to make our mission and outreach go better.

But instead of looking down on our weaknesses and lack of resources, wishing that we were as gifted in finance and personnel as larger churches, maybe we should begin to look at these limitations as a gift from God and an opportunity to attempt an incarnational approach to ministry and mission.

The Gift of Weakness

One of the most debilitating of these limitations for a small church like my own is the lack of resources. In the Presbyterian Church in Ireland's method of training its ministers, a great culture shock occurs when you finish your assistantship in a large church (because they are the ones who can afford assistants) and find yourself working in a much smaller church. This shock can be especially acute when you go into one of the small Home Mission congregations.

Moving from a large church where you felt that you were in difficulty by the time you had made your way down to the fourth pianist on the Sunday rota, it could be alarming when you discover that you have literally no one willing or able to play music or lead worship.

This was the situation I found myself in two years into my ministry in Mountmellick and Tullamore. The Mountmellick organist had stepped down due to failing eyesight and hearing and the Tullamore piano player had moved away. Sundays were difficult to say the least.

At that stage, I was musical enough to lead singing or play the guitar but certainly not sufficiently confident to do both. My guitar was sitting in the church one weekday when I opened up for a couple of Polish painters who were doing some work for us. One of the painters asked if I would mind if he played the guitar. He picked it up and began to play in a wonderful classical guitar style.

Without thinking too much about this, I went to the cupboard and took out a book of worship songs and asked if he could play the songs in the book. He opened a page at random and began sight-reading the piano music, adapting it to the guitar on the spot.

With a great deal of fervent prayer, matched only by the amount of worry in my heart about all the things that could go wrong, I then asked him if he could play for us on a Sunday. We would have nothing to pay him; it would be entirely voluntary. It might also take a bit of adjusting on his part and that of the congregation. Even with that rather downbeat sales pitch, he agreed straight away on the condition that he could bring along his son to translate for him. For two years, this father and son helped out on Sundays until work commitments began to get in the way. This was a time of outreach and connection with the local Polish community, something that would not have happened were it not for our lack of ability musically. It also blossomed out into a connection with many of the local bands.

We found out later there was a sense of disbelief that this man had begun to go to church. In broken English at a prayer meeting, he told us he was thankful that we had accepted him. His reputation on the music scene was as a hard drinking hell-raiser and his nickname, up until that time, had been the Polish equivalent of "Beelzebub." The Gospels contain a number of examples of this kind of "strength-through-weakness" approach in the ministry of Jesus. In John 4, Jesus had sent His disciples away and stopped for some much-needed rest near a well in Samaritan territory. He was thirsty and tired, and lacked the necessary equipment to draw water from the well. He was also somewhat helpless. Rather than being a hindrance to His ministry, His lack of the proper tools and personnel, in addition to His own need for water, proved to be a strength.

At exactly the wrong time of day for the heavy, difficult work of gathering water, a woman arrived and Jesus broke religious, social and cultural barriers by asking her for help. This encounter ended with a Samaritan village putting their faith in Jesus.

The story shows us how Jesus uses the physical limitations placed on Him by His incarnation as an opportunity for mission. I am sure it would be a simple, if slightly disheartening, exercise for many of us to list the weaknesses and areas of difficulty in our own ministries. Starting with our own lack of expertise and working our way out to the churches and organisations we are involved in, we might be able to come up with a long list of barriers we face and resources we lack.

What if we did such an exercise but rather than getting downhearted and seeing these limitations as barriers to our work, we saw them as opportunities to live out the weakness that comes with incarnational ministry?

We have no musicians but who can we turn to in our community for help?

We feel called to help with homelessness in our town but we do not have the numbers and the money to do this. Who can we partner with outside of the church to help us?

What the story of the Samaritan woman at the well shows us is that in looking for groups or people to collaborate with, we need not limit ourselves to churches or Christian organisations. In Samaria, Jesus' 'mission partner' was an abused abandoned female outcast. The results were spectacular.

The Gift of Place

How do we find these local people to partner with? This brings us to another of the limitations of incarnation – the limitations of geography.

As we saw earlier, the ministry of Jesus took place in an area about one-third of the size of Ireland. It did not have to be that way. Early on at the start of His ministry, a famous figure offered Him all of the kingdoms of the world along with all of their authority and splendour. Thankfully, Jesus turned down the offer.

Many of our churches are named after the area in which they are situated. Even those with saint's names or other more poetic names have a comma and a town or street placed after them. I am the minister of Mountmellick Presbyterian Church and Tullamore Presbyterian Church.

As well as being a functional way of naming a congregation, it is also a simple way of spelling out the broad mission of that church. We exist to share the gospel of Jesus in Mountmellick or in Tullamore.

Other opportunities might present themselves for overseas mission or joining together with others in all-Ireland work but this should not distract from the fact that in our name and in our calling, we are churches that seek to serve and witness to these two communities. And in order to witness in these places, we have to know the community and be part of it.

We looked earlier at the idea of movement and direction expressed by John in the eternal relationship of the Father and of the Son. What does such an abstract idea have to do with the local and geographically limited nature of the ministry of Jesus?

John paints a wonderful word image of ever decreasing circles as Jesus comes into firstly, the world, secondly, His own nation, thirdly, those willing to receive Him. Then, in the centre of this decreasing geographic and demographic circle Jesus literally "pitches His tent" among us.[9] The word that we translate as "dwelt" (ἐσκήνωσεν eskenosen) means to pitch a tent and carries with it the image from the end of the book of Exodus of the tabernacle of God right in the heart of the camped circles of His people in the wilderness.

If the direction of the eternal Logos (Word of God) is towards the heart of the Father then the direction of the incarnate Jesus is right into the centre of the community, the people among whom He has pitched His tent. He lived the life of a Jewish peasant, learned the languages and customs from His mother and Joseph, ate the same food, cried with the same sorrows and laughed at the same jokes.

In our individualistic world, we can hide behind our own front doors, watch TV from our own part of the world, in our own language or accent, drink from our own tap and eat our own favourite foods every night. We can lose sight of the fact that for Jesus, incarnation meant drinking from the same well water as the rest of the village, attending the same synagogue, eating the same crops and animals from the same fields and using the same toilets as everyone else.

What about us and our churches? Are we part of the community or do we live in a separate church culture?

• • •

Knowing Your Community

Ballina

By Marian Edwards and Emma Bolster Rodrigues

For a message to make sense to any group, it has to be explained within their context, in symbols they will understand. In other words, whether teaching, preaching, evangelising, helping or living life, mission has to be undertaken in ways the local community can relate to and appreciate. And to do that, we need to understand and appreciate the local community, its unique history and characteristics.

Ballina is a picturesque and bustling town on the north Mayo coast. Every year, fishermen travel here from all over the world in search of the king of fish, the wild Atlantic salmon. Situated on the famous River Moy, Ballina is celebrated as the salmon capital of Ireland.

The salmon is revered for its uncanny ability to travel from the deep ocean to the same river where it was born. It swims from the salty waters of the Atlantic Ocean to the fresh waters of the River Moy. The fishing season lasts from the beginning of February to the end of September, and in the month of July, the people of Ballina celebrate the annual Salmon Festival.

A visitor to these parts can explore many remote sandy beaches, the towering sea stack of Dun Briste at Downpatrick Head and Belleek Woods, which is one of the finest wooded areas in Mayo.

Situated just 20 kilometres from Ballina is the townland of Foghill. The name is a modern anglicised form of the Irish *Fo Choill,* meaning "under the wood." According to tradition, this is the place where St. Patrick was reputed to have visited the wood of Voclut or Foclut (now pronounced Foghill). It was from here that he dreamt and heard his call to Ireland, "The voice of those who were in the Wood of Voclut, which is near the western sea, and they cried out thus ... 'We entreat thee holy youth to come' ... And I was pricked to the heart ... Thanks be to God, after many years the Lord has granted to them according to their cry."[10]

Christianity took strong roots in this area and nearby are several attractive and well-preserved religious sites at Rosserk Friary (Franciscan), Moyne Abbey, Rathfran Abbey and Ballina's Augustine Abbey, all bearing witness to the area's rich Christian heritage.

In partnership with the Church of Ireland diocese of Tuam, Killala and Achonry and Church Army, Ballina Churches Together launched the Centre of Mission in 2016 as a sign of their common Christian commitment and purpose. Emma was appointed as Lead Evangelist and she began the work by building bridges with the local community. Later in 2018, Marian moved into the town as a Church Army Pioneer Evangelist.

The project needed to start where people were. That required a knowledge of the area historically and the sensitivities arising from the Achill Island Mission Colony.[11] The controversial mission and conversions among the natives of Achill during the famine gave rise to the term *souperism*, the allegation that people were offered material benefits to change their religion. We needed to be sensitive to this legacy.

We also looked at the current demographics. The town has a fragmented community with several groups experiencing poverty and exclusion alongside intergenerational unemployment and stigmatisation. 10% of Ballina's 10,171 residents come from the Traveller community. There are three housing estates which are classed as deprived and disadvantaged, with St. Patrick's Estate on the west of the town listed as one of the most disadvantaged in the country in the Pobal HP Deprivation Index 2016.[12]

Becoming Part of Your Community

But it was not enough to research, to understand and to appreciate our town. We needed to become part of this community. And we did that by participating. We took part in the various events and festivals from the St. Patrick's Day Parade to the annual Salmon Festival and the switching on of the Christmas lights.

Such celebrations meant that the streets were packed with people and our team of volunteers were soon busy face painting, making crafts and chatting with families. Since launching our Big Blue Bus as a mobile drop-in centre and café, this became a focal point. During special events it is usually parked outside the Jackie Clarke Museum, at the request of Mayo County Council.

Emma supported local initiatives such as Ballina Training Centre (Mental Health and Disabilities), MABS (the Money Advisory Budgeting Service) and Diversity Mayo (supporting refugees and migrants). Her husband Robson began to give Futsal lessons in the local GAA halls and sports halls in the area. And Marian started volunteering with the St. Vincent de Paul Charity Shop, Food Bank and Pastoral Care Team and with Foróige.

Emma built connections with the Irish Bishops' Drugs Initiative, a Catholic Church agency providing educational programmes about the danger of drugs and alcohol misuse. She also collaborated with the HSE in training volunteers in suicide prevention skills (ASIST Programme).

Participation in all these local community services and charities helped us to be involved in the lives of the people of the town. Through volunteering and service, we met many people and gained a deeper understanding of the needs of the community.

A Ministry of Presence

During the Covid-19 lockdown, we could not use the Big Blue Bus. Many of the people we know struggled with the new reality and the changes it brought. We were created for relationship, and loneliness and isolation affect people deeply. Some were afraid and others struggled with the uncertainty that the future holds. So, how could we bring Jesus to the people? How could we minister to those on the streets?

I (Marian) discovered the joy of street ministry, leaving the car at home and walking the streets of Ballina. So much of ministry starts with simply being there – being present. Sometimes simply sharing a cup of tea or a bag of chips with someone. I connect and am present in the lives of all that I meet – seeking to acknowledge the incredible worth of each person. It is a "ministry of smiles."

One thing I have noticed, on the streets of Ballina, is a sense of community amongst some of the local characters – they all know each other.

Harry would often visit us on the Big Blue Bus. He loved to come for a chat and a cup of tea. Sometimes he feels a bit depressed. He is always in town, hanging around Costa. Everyone seems to know him and it is interesting to observe the community which he is a part of. There is a sense of caring, of generosity and kindness between the different characters.

This is something that I have never noticed before and I feel somewhat challenged by it – what are we missing as Christians in our churches when out on the streets, in the market places, sitting on the benches and in the cafés, there are people who need to know about the love of God? Too often we have stayed within the four walls of our church buildings and thought this was ok. But where would Jesus be?

We see Jesus immersed in the lives of people. He went to their weddings. He met people in their everyday situations. He spent time with 'sinners' and even invited Himself to a tax collector's house. He travelled with His disciples, eating, talking, sharing stories and laughing together. It was an intimate experience of presence that encompassed every aspect of life. He mixed with people from every level of society. He ate with Pharisees and those shunned by society, the prostitutes and tax collectors.

If we are to be like Him, we need to be present in people's lives, to live incarnationally. We need to feel their pain, to share their joy and to create a space for mission "that fits seamlessly into the ordinary rhythms of life, friendships and community, and is thus thoroughly contextualised."[13]

One example of this happened when Diversity Mayo, an organisation working with Syrian refugees, asked Ballina Churches Together to support local Syrian families. I (Emma) began by teaching a few of the women English in their homes. This is how my connection with Rima came about. She is a young Syrian mother with two children, now separated from her husband after they had relationship difficulties. Rima found living in Ballina isolating but says anything is better than living through a war and the threat of being killed. A few weeks ago, she mentioned that we (another volunteer and I) are the only people who help her. Without us, she would be alone here. We are being Jesus in this situation; touching her life through love and acceptance, being there for her and listening to her.

• • •

Embracing Presence

William, Marian and Emma have embraced an incarnational approach to mission in two different contexts, a mid-sized town in County Offaly and a small town in County Mayo. They participate fully in their local communities and are present in people's lives. One recurring theme they mention is Jesus' manifesto from Luke 4. The Messiah comes to bring good news to the poor, to bind up the broken-hearted and to proclaim freedom for the captives.

Since Pentecost, the church has been anointed by the Holy Spirit with this same outward focus. The Lord of the Harvest sends us out to bring good news to the poor, the marginalised, single parents, the immigrant and the refugee. To comfort the heartbroken, bringing joy and hope to those who struggle with mental health issues, fear and anxiety, to those crushed by life's circumstances, sorrows and griefs. To proclaim freedom for those who are trapped in addiction or violence, empowering the oppressed, the shunned, the excluded, the wretched and the self-loathing.

Jesus gives us vivid illustrations to explain this kingdom style of living that is good news for the whole of life. Many kingdom parables describe the effect of presence. Yeast is mixed throughout the dough in order to bring about transformation.[14] Salt can only bring flavour healing and preservation when it is sprinkled over the food.[15] And light, when uncovered, illuminates the entire room.

Under the Old Covenant, God brought His people out of Egypt. They were called to be holy just as the Lord their God is holy.[16] That meant being completely separate from other nations so that they were not contaminated by the idolatry and sinful practices that were so prevalent. We came to understand that concept all too well during the pandemic. In order to stay safe, we were told to remain separate and "socially distant." But I would suggest that many Christians were already living a bit like that even before Covid-19. Too often the walls of our church buildings were a barrier, separating us from the wider community.

Jesus ushers in a New Covenant. While recognising our problem - sin is still a destructive virus that destroys lives - He arrives as one who is not only immune but can pass on that immunity to others. Instead of being contaminated by contact with the 'unclean' leper, Jesus makes him clean.

And Jesus calls His people to be like Him, to do what He does. His people should not be contained and hidden away in homes and church buildings but rather dispersed throughout society to incarnate the Kingdom and usher it into each unique context.

There is a pivotal moment in the history of the early church when persecution broke out and the believers were scattered throughout Judea and Samaria. And a wonderful thing happened. "Those who had been scattered preached the word wherever they went."[17]

When every believer is empowered for mission wherever they go, then God's kingdom will grow and multiply. Someone once introduced themselves to Andrew saying, "I'm a secret agent from God cunningly disguised as a schoolteacher."

I long to see Jesus followers who are present in every neighbourhood, workplace, school or college, "loving out loud" as powerful agents of transformation.[18]

I long to see churches at the heart of their community that are full of grace and truth as they embody the message they teach.[19]

Immanuel, you stepped into our world bringing light and life. As your body on earth, may we be so present in the lives of those we encounter, so that they can smell the aroma of Christ.

Take Time to Ponder

1. Where are you? What is your sphere of influence? What does it mean for you to be part of your community? Are you participating fully or are you living in a separate Christian culture?

2. Jesus was in the world but not of it. He was a true Israelite but also exposed the difference between man-made traditions and God's Kingdom. What does it mean to be in your community but not of it? What do we accept and conform to? What do we question or reject?

3. If Jesus appeared in your town today, where would you find Him? Who would He be hanging out with? What illustrations (parables) would He be using to teach people about the Kingdom of God?

4. Is your church embedded in the community or more of a 'commuter' church? Would anyone notice if you were not there?

5. List the things that you might consider weaknesses or limitations in yourself or your congregation. How might these be considered as a gift from God? What opportunities might arise from these limitations or weaknesses?

CHAPTER TWO

Mercy

"I have come that they may have life and have it to the full." John 10:10

Just a five minute walk from my home in Buncrana is a hidden gem I did not value or enjoy until a global pandemic forced me to stay within a two-kilometre radius of where I live. Concealed at the side of a stone bridge is a set of steep steps many fail to notice as they hurry past. Here the Mill River cascades down a series of rocky terraces into a deep pool and on into the last, lazy stretch before reaching the sea. Once the millrace (the channel for the water wheel), this is now free from the trappings of industry, save for the ruined mill buildings on the far bank, overgrown with shrubs and ivy.

Descending the steps feels like diving into an underwater kingdom. Guarded by ranks of fragrant pine trees, the winding pathway is bathed in flickering green light as the sun filters through a layered canopy of sycamore, ash, hawthorn and birch. Birdsong is almost drowned out by the sound of the rapids. The riverbank is draped with delicate ferns and wild garlic, interspersed with bursts of fireweed.

Edging the pathway is a stone wall, topped with jutting slabs of rock like the back of a stegosaurus and an ancient stone bench is overgrown with a velvet blanket of emerald moss. If there are 40 shades of green in

Ireland, every one of them must be represented in this vibrant mini paradise that is just sparkling with life. It feels like a deep breath.

Here it is easy to take an imaginary step into the Garden of Eden, and to ponder how the Lord of all Creation is the source of all things; the eternal I Am - Father, Son and Holy Spirit - overflowing with life and love. Surrounded by trees, growing by a stream, my mind takes me to the centre of the garden where God invites mankind to participate in the eternal, glorious, flourishing, purposeful, loving and fruitful relationship of the Trinity by tasting the fruit of the tree of life.

This was always the intention: men and women in perfect harmony with God, with each other and with Creation. Jesus says, "I have come to give life and life in all its fullness."[1] He beckons us into the fullness of Him who fills everything in every way.[2]

As I turn to leave my little taste of heaven, an ugly discord wrecks the moment. Fresh black spray paint on the brick wall of the abandoned mill screams a cruel racist message. The words drip with hatred and disdain, mirrored by the streaks of paint that have run down the wall. Here is a stark reminder of paradise lost. Instead of the tree of life, we chose the tree of death - the knowledge of good and evil.

This is the ultimate temptation, to exchange abundant life in relationship with the source of all life, for self-rule. We want to be like God by taking on God's position as judge and defining for ourselves, and for others, what is right and what is wrong. It is a knowledge that is too much for us. We do not have the capacity to judge rightly because, unlike God, we cannot perceive the thoughts of people's hearts; we can only observe the external.

Like the graffiti artist judging himself superior because of the lighter pigment in his skin, as mankind breaks relationship with the Creator, all other relationships are damaged. The consequences are shame and blame, separation, suffering and conflict.

When we take it upon ourselves to determine right from wrong, embracing the tree of the knowledge of good and evil, the result is death. We see that almost immediately in the story of Cain and Abel.[3]

As we journey through the scriptures, God's righteous law brings respite; restraining the excesses and pointing forward to a better way. But even good laws can be twisted. Paul talks of the difference between the letter and the spirit of the law.[4] By the time of Jesus, ordinary people found themselves at the mercy of elites - the 'experts' and religious leaders who defined the rules according to their own interpretation and placed unbearable burdens on the shoulders of others without lifting a finger to help, and the corrupt rulers and secular authorities who manipulated the rules to abuse people for their own selfish gain.[5]

Some were proud, superior and self-righteous as they achieved standards they themselves had defined. Others were crushed with shame and worthlessness as they were 'set at naught' by failed expectations.

And finally into this bleak and barren wilderness flows living water. Jesus steps into the pain and brokenness of shattered lives and fractured relationships, bringing life, love and freedom. At last, the desert begins to blossom. He invites people back into a flourishing and fruitful relationship with the Father, the source of all life, through His own self-giving love.

Why is this important? As we consider the postures of mission for contemporary Ireland, this one strikes a chord deep into our cultural baggage. We have described it as "mercy" - a style of ministry that is life-giving rather than judgemental, not pointing the finger of condemnation and blame but rather walking alongside people in the process of healing, forgiveness and transformation.

A Plea for Mercy

When we take upon ourselves the role of judge, we are choosing the tree of the knowledge of good and evil because we reject the one true judge, the source of life. A 'gospel' of regulations, of outward adherence to a moral code is not good news to anyone. It brings death. And yet so often this has been the message of the church, and in particular of the Irish church. It was this emphasis on morality that allowed so many to turn a blind eye to the Magdalene Laundries, Industrial Schools and Mother and Baby Homes of our modern history.

In the wake of the 2009 Ryan Report into child abuse in Industrial Schools, Irish Times Journalist Kate Holmquist wrote, "Ireland remains a shame-based society where the victim is again victimised by speaking out.. We have inherited a shame-based culture of secrecy, where truth-telling means humiliation, and it stretches into every area of life."[6]

You do not have to look far to find rampant examples on social media and in the comment section of online newspapers. And sadly, among the vocal keyboard warriors pointing fingers and heaping shame and judgement, are those who describe themselves as Christians.

According to research by the Barna Group nearly nine out of ten (87%) of young Americans felt that the word 'judgemental' accurately described modern day Christianity.[7] In our own VOX magazine survey of Young Adults in 2015, we asked church-going Millennials in Ireland what three things concerned them most about the church. The top answer was 'judgemental attitudes' (44%) followed closely by 'hypocrisy' (33%) and 'irrelevance' (31%). [8]

Why is it that those who claim to follow Jesus are best known for judgmentalism when we say we believe in the One who brings life in all its fullness? I would suggest that too often, like the Pharisees, we have clung to the tree of the knowledge of good and evil. And this tendency has damaged the witness of the church. This 'forbidden fruit' is so attractive because it offers the illusion of control. We get to determine who is in and who is out, according to our own evaluation of what matters most - whether behaviour or belief, principles or propositions.

One insightful anonymous contributor to the VOX survey in 2015 put it this way: "For my generation, Christianity and the good news has become synonymous with social and cultural conservatism. We have become known for what we are against but not what we positively represent. Mission is not about getting people to conform to a set of rules (many of which come from the sensibilities of a previous generation and not necessarily thoughtful reflection upon the Christian narrative's impact on culture today)."

Another commentator said, "Telling people they are wrong or sinning, doesn't help them but only serves to alienate them further from the supposed reality of a loving God. It makes them feel inadequate or spoiled and not worthy of a relationship with God or not deserving to be part of a church community."

How do we speak life not death to the people we meet? How can we engage, Jesus-style, with the outcast in such a way that streams of living water flow in them and through them? We need a shift in posture from judgement to mercy.

In more than ten years of ministry among students with the Christian organisation Agape, Chloe Hanan has learnt the importance of speaking life rather than judgement. She is passionate about sharing the gospel of Jesus Christ and walking with students as they grow in their faith. She explores why this principle of mercy is so vital for mission and shares stories of what this style of ministry looks like in her context.[9]

• • •

Bringing Life on Campus

Dublin and Cork

By Chloe Hanan

It is so important to challenge the concept of Christianity as an adherence to a set of rules. So often Christianity is synonymous with judgement. People need to know what it means to follow Jesus and it is not about "sin management." Sin is not a list of things we do wrong that we have to tally up at the end of the day, check and recheck in some sort of ridiculous Santa Claus situation. I come across this view a lot. In this picture, God is what Brennan Manning describes as the "niggling customs officer" rifling through our moral baggage, sorting the good from the bad.[10] We cannot possibly live under such a regime. It is soul destroying.

We have proved this throughout our generations in Ireland as we have sought to break free from oppressive rule, whether political or religious, with a suitably rebellious 'no' to living under the thumb of organised control.

In the Bible, the most common term for 'sin' comes from the Greek word meaning "to miss the mark" in the sport of archery. When someone shoots at the target and misses the bullseye, the distance from the arrow to the bullseye is called the sin. The Bible says all have sinned and fallen short. This is not a blanket of condemnation: this is a ground leveller. We are all separated. There is no elite 'in' crowd. It is a state of our heart.

Let me break it down a little more - Chloe aged seven, is told she is too fat and ugly to be loved. Powerful words took root as I believed them to be true. This is a belief that would shape my life, my choices, my behaviour and my relationships for the next ten to 15 years, infiltrating how I saw myself and the world. This belief is the complete antithesis to the Bible, which declares a love more powerful than death where God knows the number of hairs on my head.

I am not a Disney fan but I am a rescue fan: I love me a gutsy happy ending. And in this story, sin does not get to win. Jesus was the ultimate rescuer. He went to the depths, pulled the plug on sin and its consequences, and now holds the key.

Too often, I was afraid to ask all the questions I had about pain and suffering because I did not know if God was big enough for them. This is a cul-de-sac many Christians go down and fail to come out of. It is a dead end for faith, as there seems nowhere to go. It was the Psalms that drew me out of that fear, as they let loose, held nothing back and let out full steam at God. So I have left my timid, fearful, no-questions-asked faith, where there is so much under the carpet you cannot move. I have questioned. I have approached the edge of that cliff and stood on it.

This is so important for my generation. We can now walk up to doubt and ask the tough questions. The paradoxes that seem to undermine belief are actually at the heart of vibrant faith. But it is only by continually wrestling with them, rather than pinning down or pushing away, that faith is seen, realised and lived.

Love Not Judgement

Call it stress relief, but I have recently discovered a love for boxing - watching men 'bate' the heads off each other. There is something about the sheer strength those men have, the ability to raise a fist and thump one another with a power that brings them to their knees and flattens them out, sometimes unconscious at their feet and then the roar of the crowd as they lift their hands in victory that has me hooked.

Christian judgement is a bit like a boxing match. Regardless of your ability to throw a punch literally, as a Christian you hold within your power a potential to knock out those in your community. Just as world heavyweight champion, Anthony Joshua goes in with a right handed jab, adds a left counterpunch with a looping hook, and finishes off with a right uppercut that slams his opponent into a knockout, Christian judgement has a three-pronged attack.

1. You have done something wrong
2. I reject you - I will no longer accept you or associate with you
3. I am right to do this (generally because I have the moral high ground)

The blow that comes from such judgement is profound and long lasting. It brings people to their knees, often knocking them out entirely. I have been both the executor and the recipient of these knockouts. I have had the moral high ground and presided over the conquest of those beneath me. I have also been on the receiving end. When already on my knees in life, I have experienced the three-pronged attack of having my brokenness seen and rejected, and I have watched the superior look in someone's eyes as they walked away from me. It floored me.

Risking that judgement is a profound fear I still live with. It keeps me silent about my brokenness with people. To ask the already-pained heart to endanger itself with more rejection is a last-straw situation.

For the past ten years, I have worked with the student organisation, Agape. Part of my job involves sharing life and building community with young adults, investing in their lives and then calling them into missional opportunities with their friends. Judgement is something that I come across a lot. There is so much suffering in people's varied experiences of being judged. It is a systemic problem that causes the witness of believers to falter and be powerless.

Paul Reid was the first person I heard explain this, but you may have heard it elsewhere: the 'Behave, Believe, Belong' culture Christianity has created. You have to behave this way, so we know you believe what we do and then you can belong with us. If we desire authenticity, we will reject this. And rightly so, because it is not what Jesus modelled to us.

He had a unique way of drawing people in. He did not take offence at people's brokenness. Instead He looked with mercy. You see it in the way He dealt with each person that approached Him. Jesus draws them into conversation. He does not deal with the behaviour first, He gets to the heart. He invited people into relationship (belonging), and then called them to believe in Him. Only then could behaviour be addressed as the working out of this new found belief in the Son of God, who is their rescuer, king, friend and saviour, and the in-working of the Holy Spirit.

In His teaching, Jesus turns the culture of judgement on its head. In Matthew's gospel there is an extensive account of teaching from the Sermon on the Mount. "Judge not, that you be not judged. For with what judgment you judge, you will be judged; and with the measure you use, it will be measured back to you."[11] This is not metaphorical, this is Ronseal.

It does exactly what it says on the tin.

Matthew Henry defines judgement as "the setting of someone to naught."[12] Reducing someone to zero. Putting them so far down that they are no longer a person.

Jesus' instruction is as clear as day. Do not judge. Do not make the worst of people. Do not infer insidious things from their actions or their words. Do not judge their state by a single act, or by who they have been to you. It is God's prerogative to test the heart, to examine our intentions and motivations, our words and our actions. It is not our job to step onto His throne. There is only one judge. He is judge of all the earth and He will do right.[13]

Jesus warns of some serious consequences for those who do judge - according to the law of retaliation. What would become of us should God start judging us with the same severity we execute over someone else's mistakes?

The rest of Jesus' teaching was familiar to me as a Sunday school kid. (Do not try to take a speck of sawdust out of your brother's eye if you have a whopping great plank of wood in your own). The art of reproving - speaking the truth in love to others - is not for the faintheart. And it is not for everyone. It is not for those who themselves are guilty of the faults of which they accuse others.

Jesus teaches us to deal with our own house first. As God changes my heart and goes after the sin that separates me from Him, I become so much more aware of myself and I understand that I am a sinner who is greatly loved. Recognising our own sin doesn't excuse us from addressing what we see with someone else. We cannot sit back in apathy as someone walks towards a cliff edge. For me, mission is about leading people to Jesus, and that is done in the context of love and truth.

We need to create a place of safety where people know they are accepted and loved unconditionally. Only then can I sit opposite a student who is telling me the horror and pain they have experienced - whether from an abortion, sexual assault, their own drunken behaviour, an STD or the abuse of a parent. When someone feels safe to share what they are ashamed of, at that moment my response is not to try and control or 'fix' it but to whisper a prayer, "Jesus, help me see what is going on in the heart."

When I was working with toddlers, we knew that often their behaviour was an indication of a deeper problem. We would step back from the tantrum and ask, "What is going on here? Are they tired? Hungry? Hurting?" If I am more concerned about the rules than I am about the person, I will not be able to sit with someone in their brokenness. Jesus met people where they were, without condemnation and called them into relationship with Himself.

So what happens when I am faced with Jenny, a student who has a serious problem with promiscuous sex? My human reaction is to fix and control. I know this is destructive behaviour. I want to shake her. But Jesus stops me from doing that and says, "Just listen."

And when she finally tells me the full horror of the vicious sexual assault that began this cycle of self-harm, Jesus asks me to sit with her in her pain; to understand that her behaviour is a desperate attempt to regain control and to find a way to numb the pain. And He prompts me to tell her I love her.

This is not black and white Christianity. We have the idea that when someone starts to follow Jesus they are suddenly transformed into this glorious human being. The reality is so different. If we are unable to sit with people in their pain, if we are shocked because we are holding on to a moral rule that is more important than the person in front of us, then we will never be able to do mission.

Jesus says, "And when He [the Holy Spirit] has come, He will convict the world of sin, and of righteousness, and of judgment."[14] The Holy Spirit will convict the world of sin. Let that sink in. Conviction is His job, not ours.

That does not mean that we can never confront destructive patterns, but it does mean we step back from trying to control behaviour. We do not abandon people to the isolation of causation. And at the right time, in the context of well-established relationship, we can begin to help them see the truth and point them to the source of life and healing.

Connecting

On Campus, we reach out to students by doing a simple five-minute survey with them about God. We are totally up-front that we are a Christian organisation and the survey often leads to great conversations. So many of the students really want to talk. Sometimes we never see them again. At other times, they may connect with us through Facebook or come along to an event or a retreat.

It is a slow process. We met Jason while doing a survey and he kept coming back to talk with us. He joined us on the Camino Way. Five years later, on his fourth Camino, he suddenly announced one evening, "I have decided to become a Christian." If we were in this for the statistics, we would be done already. We are certainly not hitting any sales targets. But there is such joy in seeing Jesus moving in people's lives.

Throughout the year, small groups of students continue to meet to have discussions about faith and go deeper with their relationship with Jesus. Sometimes we meet with them on-to-one. We share 'pathways of wonder' - beautiful treasures we have found in the Scriptures to encourage and inspire them. We want to encourage them to read the Bible for themselves and to let the word of God do its work in their lives.

Walking Side by Side

Every year, we invite a mixed group of students to join us on the Camino Way. In the early years, I was not enthusiastic. I rolled my eyes at the thought of the 160 kilometre trek but went anyway. The group included some who were Christians and others who wanted to join for the adventure. The Camino is daunting. It is a physical challenge and a shared experience that creates a new dynamic between people. We are achieving something together, sharing meals, walking side by side and relaxing together in the evenings. It creates opportunities for relationship and conversation.

On the first day, I found myself walking with Emily who had a Christian boyfriend but had been nervous of joining the trip because she felt very much on the outside. But we got on like a house on fire and in the first hour, she really opened up. We discovered that we had a profound shared experience and that made her feel safe.

Susan, who was also dating a Christian, had a negative experience of church. She knew that other Christians were judging her. She came to me and said, "I want to read the Bible because I want to understand for myself what it says." I said, "Absolutely, I am totally happy to do that with you." So I met with her each week and we began to read through John's gospel together. Gradually, Jesus introduced Himself to her through the pages of the gospel. She began to see past the baggage of religion to who Jesus was.

Later, she joined us on the Camino and one night she said, "This might sound weird but I feel like I have started a relationship with God." I let her set the pace of our journey together and the Holy Spirit did His work to bring her to Jesus.

• • •

Embracing Mercy

Chloe has described how her ministry with Agape is shaped by this principle of mercy. Studying the stark contrast between the merciful, life-giving ministry of Jesus and the crushing impact of judgement, reveals important lessons that are so relevant to mission in contemporary Ireland.

You have heard the term 'guilt by association.' The Pharisees regularly criticised and condemned Jesus for the people He rubbed shoulders with. On one memorable occasion, Jesus encountered a tax collector named Matthew and said, "Follow me."[15] Tax collectors are never the most popular of people but in Bible times the profession was notoriously corrupt and tainted by traitorous collaboration with the Roman Empire.

Surely Matthew's immediate obedience should be a cause for celebration? Here is someone who is choosing to turn away from his murky past and begin a journey of faith. He even opens his home to introduce Jesus to all his friends and colleagues. His hospitality provides a wonderful gospel opportunity for Jesus to interact with a whole new set of people. Yet the Pharisees respond with condemnation, "Why does your teacher eat with tax collectors and sinners?"[16]

These were the experts, the ones whose job was to teach others about God, and yet they did not know God or understand His ways. The "gracious and compassionate God" of the Jewish Scriptures was standing in front of them, and they did not recognise Him.[17]

Jesus challenges them, "It is not the healthy who need a doctor, but the sick. But go and learn what this means: 'I desire mercy, not sacrifice.' For I have not come to call the righteous but sinners."[18]

The tree of knowledge separates and divides right from wrong, good from bad, healthy from sick, but the kingdom of God infiltrates and transforms. The radiance of life and light banishes darkness. Here the principle of mercy intersects with that of incarnation or presence. Is it time to review our social calendars? How much time do we spend associating with the 'right' people when the kingdom opportunities might be somewhere else entirely? What stops us being a friend to those who others reject?

In Ballina, Marian Edwards describes a friendship she has developed with a number of Traveller women. "I would never have engaged with Travellers before I came to Ballina," she admits. But now a deepening friendship with a number of women has enriched her life.

"The Bible has a lot to say about caring for widows but today I think the widows in our society include single mothers. One Traveller woman I know has three children. Her husband died in suspicious circumstances and like many Travellers, she has not remarried out of respect for the memory of her husband. As a single mum, she struggles with many issues and one of these is self-esteem. This woman already has a deep faith and talks about God. It reminds me that Jesus comes to bind up the broken-hearted. I love having tea with her and praying with her. When I pray, it cracks her up because it is so different to what she is used to. My hope and my prayer for her is that the Lord will heal her broken heart and show her that she is His masterpiece. He knows her and has seen all the tears that she has cried. He cares about the needs of widows and orphans."

Bringing Life Not Death

On another occasion, the Pharisees were watching to see whether Jesus would heal a man on the Sabbath.[19] Jesus asks for their interpretation of the law, "What is lawful on the Sabbath - to do good or to do evil, to save life or to kill?"[20] When they refuse to answer, Jesus is angry and *deeply distressed*.

Here is damning evidence that they would prefer the man to suffer than to bring healing and restoration. If the greatest commandment is love, they have fallen far short of the mark. Jesus heals the man and the Pharisees go out and plot to kill Him. Jesus brings life, but the knowledge of good and evil brings death.

In John 8, a woman is made to stand in front of a whole group of men. Caught 'in the act of adultery' it was quite likely that she was only partially clothed. Try to imagine what it must have been like for her. What would it be like to have the worst thought, word or action of your life put on public display? Feeling sick to her stomach, she would be desperately trying to cover her nakedness and shame. She was surrounded by a pack of wolves, all baying for her blood. Her secrets were laid bare, exposed to public comment and condemnation. But she was standing alone. Two people were in the bed but only one was dragged out. This was unjust judgement. The scales were unbalanced, loaded against her and there was no witness for the defence.

But this was not just a question of the law. The religious leaders had an ulterior motive. They were setting a trap for Jesus by presenting Him with a 'simple' matter of right and wrong. Utterly convinced of their understanding and interpretation of the law, they demanded a death sentence. For them, there was no alternative. It was obvious what should be done.

And Jesus said nothing. Instead He leant down and started to write in the sand. If the woman was pinning her hopes on an intervention, they must have started to fade. And yet, gradually the focus shifted. All eyes, once trained on the woman with self-righteous anger, now turned to look at the upstart Rabbi.

Finally, He spoke, and His words sent shock-waves through the crowd, "Let any one of you who is without sin be the first to throw a stone at her."[21] This was a verdict that satisfied justice because there was equality and balance.

He who was without sin, refused to deal in judgement (death) and instead demonstrated mercy and loving care. He covered her shame by shifting attention onto Himself - when people were looking at Him, they were not staring at her. His challenge sent her accusers away, shame-faced and silenced. And when finally He turned to her, He brought restoration. "Neither do I condemn you. Go and leave your life of sin."[22]

The hypocrisy of judgement and double standards does untold damage to the kingdom of God. We need to have our eyes open to the injustice and inequality of human judgement that looks on the outward but is unable to discern the thoughts of people's hearts; that condemns one person and gives another a free pass.

Mercy is so important in a land where shame is endemic and where unjust, unbalanced judgement is rife. We see the effects on people who have been tried and condemned based on prejudice and misinformation.

Public shaming, victim blaming, prejudice, sectarianism and racism are the fruit of the tree of knowledge.

Life-giving interactions will always re-focus people on Jesus - the source of life.

Glorious Little Things

We are all familiar with the "big" stories of the gospels but I also love the small life-giving interactions Jesus had with ordinary people. These were the brief encounters of everyday life that provide us with a glimpse of God's heart. If Jesus only does what the Father is doing, then this is the way God treats people.

He showed dignity and respect to a woman who was branded an outcast because of her menstrual bleeding. He praised a Gentile woman for her faith and persistence. He welcomed a group of children who arrived to "disrupt" His sermon. He noticed and honoured the outrageous generosity of a widow. His heart went out to a grieving mother. He wept with Mary and Martha after the death of Lazarus.

When we accuse, condemn or reject people based on what they do (or do not do) we crush and deflate them. But speak 'life' to someone and you will see an immediate impact. Their eyes will brighten. Their tension will ease. Their lungs will fill with breath. I am convinced that this principle of mercy is essential as we embrace incarnational mission in Ireland.

Gracious and compassionate Lord, you showed us mercy when we deserved judgement. Let us extend that same mercy to those around us as we introduce them to the One who brings life in all its fullness.

Take Time to Ponder

1. Why was Jesus known as the friend of sinners? What was it about Him that made people feel safe in His presence?

2. Are there distinctions between judgement and condemnation? Are there limitations in our human authority or capacity to make judgements? James 2:13 says, "Mercy triumphs over judgement." Why? How does a merciful approach enable people to experience life and true freedom? How do we create an environment that allows truth and grace to flourish? How do we build and not destroy?

3. What has love got to do with it? What are we known for as individuals or as a church community? Many have experienced harsh judgement delivered by someone who claims to be speaking "in love." When is it appropriate to speak the truth and when should we be silent?

4. What are the good (or not so good) examples from your own experience? Can you think of life-giving interactions in your own ministry that re-focused attention on Jesus?

CHAPTER THREE

Humility

"Follow me and I will make you fishers of men..." Matthew 4:19

It was just five miles from the motorway to the place I was to stay that night in rural County Down but those five miles were the most gruelling of an already marathon-like day. Ahead of me, my host drove confidently, winding through familiar-to-him country lanes.

My hands gripped the steering wheel; my eyes were fixed on the red tail lights glaring in the pitch darkness of the unlit road as I tried to keep up. Weary beyond words, I had lost track of the number of turns, my sense of direction shot to pieces by the combination of darkness and exhaustion. The thought crossed my mind, "If I lose him now, I will be utterly lost." I did not even know the address.

Thankfully, we eventually reached our destination safely, but the experience stayed with me and reminded me of something that Methodist Minister Rev. Laurence Graham said when I met him for the first time while he was working in Cork and Kerry.

"Early in my ministry, they used to talk about a five-year plan," Laurence said. "I never had any but I do not feel bad about that any more. The overwhelming sense I have had is that I am tailgating the God of Mission. I am following Jesus and just seeing which doors are opening."

Tailgating the God of Mission

Tailgating the God of Mission - allow that to sink in for a moment.

We love to have our plans and strategies, to know exactly where we are going and map out our journey. But there are times when God calls us to step out and follow Him without a map, GPS or blueprint. In those moments, Jesus calls us to a place of humility and surrender, to a quiet trust that the God of mission knows the way and He is the Lord of the Harvest. The journey may be long and gruelling, but the car in front will lead us safely to our destination.

Over our 30 years in ministry, Andrew has described this (a little less eloquently than Laurence) as "muddling along with Jesus." And although at times the adventure has been painful, frustrating, terrifying and heart-breaking, I would not change one thing.

One of the most profound lessons we have had to learn is that this is not about us. It is not our agenda, our plans, our ambitions or our strategies. And that is such a relief because neither is it about our strengths, our skills or our resources. It is *Missio Dei* - God's mission. It is about His kingdom, His purposes and His church. He is the author and perfecter of our faith. And He is more invested in seeing the fulfilment than we are.

Look at a few of the things Jesus says: "Follow me and I will make you fishers of men..."[1] "I will build my church and the gates of hell will not prevail against it..."[2] "Go into all the world and make disciples of all nations... and behold I am with you always..."[3]

First and foremost, we are called to follow Jesus. To go where He goes. To do what He does. To say what He says. That is so freeing. There is a simplicity about allowing God to lead us, to show us what He is doing and where He is working. But it is also humbling and, at times, quite scary.

When we first arrived in Ireland in 2005, we had quite a mission pedigree. For almost 15 years, we had been honing our skills, leading teams and teaching others. And yet suddenly we found ourselves in a context where all our previous experience seemed to count for nothing. I am not the first to describe it this way but for us, it felt like sowing seeds on a car park.

Our journey since then has been one of allowing God to strip away our self-reliance. When we have attempted to 'make' things happen, our efforts have been futile. But when we have relinquished control and allowed Him to take the lead, that is when we have seen exciting things.

There is a freedom in understanding that each mission field - whether it is a workplace, a community, a neighbourhood or a particular demographic - will require different approaches and styles. The common factor is not a proven strategy, a dynamic leader, a thriving congregation or a healthy bank balance. Nor is it our expertise, our knowledge and our experience.

The key is our posture - a cross-shaped, Christ-like humility that understands that God does not choose the people we would choose and He does not do things in the way we would expect.

Tailgating the God of mission will involve learning from One who is "gentle and humble of heart."[4] It will shape our attitudes and ultimately our actions as we become responsive to the prompting of the Holy Spirit. It may also have an impact on our diaries. When we are focused on programmes, meetings and events, we will not have time and space for God encounters.

Interestingly, for many people that was one of the more positive outcomes of the Covid-19 crisis. With church services, meetings and events cancelled; there was a greater freedom to stop and chat with a neighbour over the garden fence, to pray with a church member over the phone or to respond to a cry for help.

My co-authors describe similar experiences. Wonderful opportunities, open doors and seasons of fruitful ministry came when they relinquished control and followed closely behind the one who was willing to empty Himself and humble Himself (even to the point of death).[5] So this principle of humility, so closely aligned to that of incarnation, embraces the simplicity of following Jesus and allowing Him to make us 'fishers of men.' Let us look together at examples from Offaly, Mayo and Dublin.

• • •

On a Mission From God (Jesus Style)

Tullamore

By William Hayes

A few years ago, I had something of a crisis in my understanding of mission. This was a difficult thing, not least because I work as a minister in the Home Mission department of the Presbyterian Church in Ireland.

"What is mission really about?" I asked myself, and "How are we called by God to carry this out?" I decided to spend some time reading the gospels and looking to see what Jesus did when it came to reaching out. My approach was simple, look at Jesus' approach to mission and see if it can be done today. Along the way, I became more and more impressed at the sheer variety of methods and settings that Jesus used to call people to follow Him. From teaching in synagogues to meeting a man in a graveyard, disputing in the temple grounds to stopping under a tree in Jericho, Jesus seemed to use everything at His disposal to reach those around Him.

So, if I was approaching the gospels looking for simple techniques then I was going to be disappointed. Rather than one or two formulas, the gospels (and then Acts and the letters) contained a whole armoury of methods of doing mission in a Jesus-like manner. One thing stood out in the midst of this array of styles and locations. It was not so much a mission technique as a kind of 'non-technique.' Repeatedly in the gospels, Jesus finds Himself simply encountering people who are in some kind of need. These are what we might in other circumstances call, 'happy coincidences,' but I am not sure that there really is such a thing in a world governed by an omnipotent God. Let us look at a few of these 'chance' encounters and see what we can learn from them. There is a scene in the book of John in which Jesus has one of the most successful mission encounters recorded in the Gospels. Within the space of a couple of days, a whole town became believers.

What was the formula that Jesus used to reach these people? What great evangelistic tools does Jesus employ here that we might copy? The technique appears to be disarmingly simple. Firstly, find yourself tired, thirsty and alone in enemy territory. Secondly, ask the most unlikely and socially excluded person in the area for help. We could include challenging that person about one of the most painful aspects of her life, but that might be following the story a little too far.

In a different incident, Jesus goes through Jericho and stops under a tree to invite Himself into the home of an unpopular man who has made a show of Himself by climbing up that tree to see Jesus.

Again, this results in another group of unlikely people coming to faith in Jesus with clear practical results in the debt and taxation industries of the town. To find a method in this, should we be walking around looking up trees, in case there are potential converts hiding there? Jesus transforms the lives of people that the religious members of their community would have regarded as beyond redemption. No pattern can be seen in the details but, time and again, we see Jesus carrying out His mission through chance encounters.

Matthew 8 illustrates this aspect of Jesus' life vividly. It opens with a leper braving the crowd to fall before Jesus. We then see a centurion, a disciple's mother-in-law and two demon-possessed men who live in tombs approach Jesus and experience His healing and transformation in some manner. There is obviously more to this than chance encounters.

In each of these stories, Jesus is leaving Himself open to the moving of the Father, to the actions of the Spirit of God in people's lives. This is something that all of us involved in mission will have experienced at some time or other; that moment when you start out your day with one set of goals and then find your plans suddenly derailed by a person or incident. In the midst of this derailment, an opportunity suddenly presents itself to speak about Jesus or to engage in some action of kingdom-growing mercy or love. We realise at this point that God has arranged this appointment all along. Let me give two examples from my own ministry. Not long after arriving in Tullamore, we celebrated the 150th anniversary of the founding of the congregation. In honour of this, we held a complete read through of the Bible from beginning to end from Sunday evening, through the days and nights and on until late Friday morning when we finished with the last words of Revelation. Having the building open throughout the night meant that we began to have a number of homeless people come and join us for the four nights. Homelessness in Offaly is somewhat different to homelessness in the cities and larger towns of Ireland. We often have homeless people who come through Offaly and stay just a few nights on their way to somewhere else such as Galway, Dublin or Limerick. We had a few of these folks arrive and they made themselves comfortable at the back of the church.

Quite early into the proceedings, it became clear that one of the first readers was not going to turn up. A man, who shall remain nameless, was booked into a 30-minute slot near the start. Most people there were already booked into their own half hour sessions and so, I approached one of the homeless men who had appeared at the back of the church and asked him if he would be able to come forward and read.

He took out of his pocket a little leather case in which there was a beautiful pair of reading glasses. After cleaning them, he went forward and waited his turn to read a portion of Genesis.

At the end of his reading, I began to walk him over to the board on which we had marked out the reading schedule for the next five days. I told him that we should replace the name of the man on the board with his.

When I asked him his name, a bit of a shiver ran down my spine. He had the same name as the man he had replaced. I took him to the board and said, "Mr… your name is already there." It spooked him a little as well and he went for a bit of a walk before coming back to the church and becoming one of the mainstays of the readings throughout those five days. It would of course be a beautiful end to this story to talk about how the man came to faith after that time of reading and quietly talking about the Word of God. But at the end of that week he continued his journey and I have never seen him again. He took with him one of the presentation Bibles that we had purchased for those who took part and he spent a lot of time over those few days reading the Bible both publicly and quietly.

Going Nowhere?

Another chance encounter came out of a time of frustration when I felt that a particular ministry project was going nowhere. In response to the food poverty crisis in the Midlands in the years after the recession, our Church, along with a number of other local groups began to run a 'community kitchen.' This was meant to be a simple cooking together project that would operate out of the church hall and allow people to cook for one another, alleviating poverty and the loneliness that so often comes with it.

As with so many simple ideas, it turned out to be incredibly complicated to get going. The committee kept growing but little work was being done. Then the local council got involved and, with the best will in the world, everything ground to a halt. The Thursday after a particularly depressing meeting in which the project seemed to fall apart, one of the local councillors arrived during our morning prayer time.

She had seen the work being done to establish the community kitchen and wanted to ask if our church would get involved in "a refugee thing" that was going to be happening in the county. We said that if we could help we would and so I turned up to a meeting at the County Council the following week.

I was presented with a list of the names of people who would be coming to live in our town. They were from the Hazara community, a group of mostly Shia Afghans. These were a group that I had been praying for on and off for years after I had read about their difficulties in Afghanistan.

Sensing God's hand in this, I agreed straight away that, as a church, we would head up a local welcoming group to work alongside the council, find good neighbours and try to foster natural friendships for the families that would be arriving.

What followed were years of blessing as we grew close to these families, as we shared in their joys and sorrows and as they came to see our church every Thursday afternoon as their own space of peace and rest in the midst of their busy week of language classes and work training.

The community kitchen did eventually happen, years later, and provided a bridge into the Traveller community, but it was only through the links made with this 'failed' project that we were able to become so closely involved in carrying out Jesus' mandate from Matthew 25 to welcome, feed and provide neighbours to these refugees and, through them, the wider Muslim community.

The failure of the community kitchen led to a time six months later when the prayer leader at the local mosque declared publicly that we were a church that "loved Muslims."

In times afterwards, churches in other areas would ask how we became involved in so close a relationship with the council resettlement project. I did not have an adequate answer or one that could be simply replicated. Like Jesus arriving on the shore at Genesaret, we just happened to disembark at the right place at the right time. If we did one thing right, it was to see God creating a moment of opportunity and seize it with both hands.

So, how do we follow the example of Jesus and 'accidentally' find ourselves in these places in which the Spirit of God is at work? Do we stand around on street corners and wait for something to happen? Maybe. There are certainly worse church growth strategies out there. A better option might be to take Jesus' words at face value about where we will find Him.

One Sabbath day during His preaching ministry, Jesus returned home. As He was the local boy who had done well for Himself and had developed a bit of a reputation, they let Him preach. He read these words from Isaiah 61, "The Spirit of the Lord is on me because He has anointed me to proclaim good news to the poor..."[6]

The mission of Jesus has not changed. His Spirit might find a home today in places and people beyond the imaginings of His home crowd in that synagogue in Nazareth, far flung places like the cold island of Hibernia, but these words still ring true and should act for us like the wording on an old treasure map for finding Jesus. They tell us to look for the poor, the prisoners, the sick and the oppressed and there, in the midst of them, we will find Jesus.[7]

• • •

God's Fingerprints

Ballina

By Marian Edwards and Emma Bolster Rodrigues

In missiological terms, *Missio Dei* is "an expression that mission is primarily a part of who God is, rather than an activity or aspect of the Church."[8] By acknowledging the idea of *Missio Dei,* we realise that God is already at work in the world. He is already present and working in the lives of people that we encounter. It is our job to look for God's fingerprints and follow the Holy Spirit's leading.

I (Marian) love reading about Peter and I see myself reflected in his life. Brave? Brash? Crazy? Maybe a little. But he is willing to take a risk for the Lord. In a moment, he gets out of the boat and suddenly he is doing the impossible. He is walking on water. We can imagine him looking back at the other disciples and saying, "Why are ye all still in the boat? Jesus is out here."

God goes before us but sometimes we have to "get out of the boat."[9] Jesus is walking on the water and we need to be prepared to take risks in order to follow Him and join Him in what He is doing.

Jesus went through all the towns and villages on foot, meeting people, praying with people, ministering to people and doing good. Perhaps it is time to get our sandals on and follow Jesus' example. As He journeyed, He met people and those life-changing encounters took place in the most ordinary places - by the side of the road, over the dinner table and at the well.

We see something similar in the life and ministry of Paul and his companions when they "travelled to Philippi, a Roman colony and the leading city in Macedonia." On the Sabbath they went outside the city walls to find a place to pray. They sat down by the river and chatted with the women there. One was called Lydia, a prosperous businesswoman who was already worshipping God. This was a God encounter and, "The Lord opened her heart to respond to Paul's message."[10] In Philippi, there was no synagogue; no Jewish community but Paul met a foreign businesswoman in a male dominated society in an encounter by the river.

The Alpha Course

In autumn/winter 2019, we were approached by a secondary teacher from the local convent school. She had attended an Alpha Course in Sligo and was keen to run one in Ballina. (The Alpha Course is a series of interactive sessions exploring the basics of the Christian faith.)[11] We were so excited to be asked and it was an example of Missio Dei in Ballina – the Holy Spirit was leading us and opening doors.

Up to 20 people attended every week. A core group gathered to set up and spend time in prayer. Each table was decorated with table arrangements and flowers, and tea and coffee was served as people came in. We served a full meal, which consisted of a main course and home-made desserts (no sandwiches allowed). Those who came every week enjoyed the videos, the singing and the discussions. We found that people really wanted to chat, to be heard and to discuss ideas.

For the retreat day away, we organised a bus to bring everyone to Holy Hill Hermitage. This is such a special place near the Atlantic coast at Skreen in County Sligo. It is a place for reflection, home to a small community of men and women who live according to the Carmelite tradition. They welcome people of all faiths. Holy Hill offers beauty, silence and solitude where people can connect with God. The generosity of the community was amazing. They allowed us total access to their delightful house. Everyone had a memorable and blessed day.

One of the most striking things from the Alpha course was how quickly strangers became friends and how much people appreciated being able to talk and openly discuss the Bible together. It was a safe place where people could express the tough questions of life.

When I (Marian) first met Victor, he was broken and he cried a lot. His wife of 30 years had died almost one year earlier, just a week after being diagnosed with cancer. Victor's world was shattered. He struggled with shock and loneliness but had found some solace from his involvement with the Ballina Men's Shed.

Victor came along to the Alpha course and he was a great help with all the practicalities of setting up before everyone came but he was still struggling with his wife's death and he could not comprehend why God let her die. He was angry, hurt and blaming God.

Then one week, we were looking at why Jesus died and Victor had a God-moment. He saw how God the Father gave His Son for our sins, how Jesus suffered and died and how God Himself experienced suffering and death. Somehow in that moment Victor came to terms with the loss of his wife. God bound up his broken heart, restored his soul and he began to heal.

God Encounters

Michael is a member of the Traveller community. One day, I (Marian) drove into the estate and just rolled down the window of my car and spoke to this man. In God's timing, I was introduced to him again the following day.

Eventually, I got to know his wife. A friendship and trust has developed that has become very precious to me. She has great faith in God and she has become a blessing to me. Their grandchildren come to the Kids Club on board the Big Blue Bus. We send her videos and worship songs and often pray with her.

I have also discovered so many 'God encounters' while going for walks through the streets of Ballina. Without plan or agenda, I head off, responding to the prompting of God's Spirit to chat with people I meet.

Beleek Woods became a place of solace for me in the midst of the Covid-19 pandemic. It is a beautiful mixed woodland located on the western bank of the River Moy. I go there several times a week to enjoy God's amazing creation and pray. The people of Ballina are friendly, so it is not unusual to have chats with people.

One morning, I met an elderly lady and we chatted for a few moments. I was not talking to her for more than two minutes, when the conversation turned to God. It is impossible to be in such a beautiful place and not see the hand of God the Master Artist everywhere. Because of Covid-19, it is easier to have those God conversations and I have started to carry little booklets of prayers and scripture readings (*Calm for the Soul* by Ruth Gyves) so I can give them out to people I meet.

Words of Hope

At the beginning of lockdown, I (Marian) was part of a Praxis Learning Community, which met online to encourage and support one another.[12] A Danish man shared the simple idea of using chalk to write Bible verses and words of inspiration and hope on footpaths and pavements in his town. That day I went out to buy chalk but I did not have the courage to do it for several weeks. Eventually I decided to give it a go. I wrote things like, "Faith, Hope, Love," "Jesus is the light of the world," "Thank you to all frontline workers," and "Hope is being able to see there is light despite the darkness" on the footpath near the Roman Catholic Cathedral in Ballina. Many people walk past this spot every day. I added simple drawings of hearts, butterflies and a cross. There were amazing reactions from people and the whole project has grown. We have a whole team of people doing it now, including one young woman who is a gifted artist and a passionate evangelist.

One Saturday morning, I met a man who was taking photos of the chalk art. He told me he wanted to send the photos to his sister in England who has been ill with cancer and was going in for a serious operation. He was hoping the words and images would brighten her day and encourage her. He also needed encouragement himself as he was struggling with his mental health. God used these simple chalk drawings in the lives of so many people in Ballina and beyond.

• • •

Are You a Secret Millionaire?

Ringsend, Dublin

By Joe Donnelly

I love the word spontaneity. When you are on mission with God there are these spontaneous, 'lightning rod' moments. I have seen it happen so many times.

In the story of Peter and John going to the temple to pray,[13] they see a beggar sitting at the Beautiful Gate and suddenly everything just spontaneously explodes. They most likely did not get out of bed that day saying, "We are going to see that aul beggar healed today" but God did something amazing through them. There is a sense of excitement when you know that God is at work. Do we allow for that? Are we looking for those moments?

In the day-to-day tasks of running our project, we encounter all sorts of people.

Sarah helps with the running of the local Chapel. She called to our centre to buy some flowers and, in the course of our conversation, she mentioned that she had an awkward question to ask me. I sensed that she was a little bit uneasy and so I said, "You can ask me anything you want, don't feel awkward."

She went on to say that some local people were wondering if my wife and I were secret millionaires. Her question took me completely by surprise, you could have scraped me off the floor. I had never suspected anyone would consider us in those terms.

To buy me some time, I asked her why she was asking this question. She said, "Whenever the various community groups need help with painting or gardening or whatever, you and your wife arrive with a team of volunteers to help and do a great job and you don't charge any money. As well as that, everyone knows about you going to places in the third world to help the poor. People are saying that you must be secret millionaires."

I felt a unique opportunity was presenting itself and so I admitted that I was indeed a secret millionaire but that she wasn't to tell anyone. "I knew it," she said, "Was it the lottery?"

I told her that I had inherited my wealth from my Father. She nearly choked as she replied, "Don't be ridiculous, we all know that your father is over 40 years dead and he left your poor mother penniless to raise eight children."

I answered by saying, "I am a secret millionaire because I am spending the fabulous wealth of my Father's inheritance." As I was saying these words, I was pointing up to the sky and I could see that the truth of what I was saying was beginning to dawn on Sarah.

She was struggling to find words and simply said, "I think that is the most beautiful thing I have ever heard."

• • •

Embracing Humility

As William, Marian, Emma and Joe shared examples from their contexts, I wonder what thoughts were going through your mind? Does it all seem too simple? Naïve perhaps? The point of this chapter is not that everyone immediately starts going for walks (although to be fair, that is not such a bad idea), writing chalk messages or organising Bible-reading marathons. Tailgating the God of mission starts with you and me simply and humbly following Jesus.

My own examples are more likely to involve failures or food. Failures because unlike Joe, I do not have the knack of turning any conversation effortlessly and seamlessly to spiritual truths. When I encountered an almost identical question in our community ("Are you secret millionaires?") my response was stuttering and floundering rather than inspired.

And food, because I have learnt that God does not ask us to become someone else. In my case I have had to accept that I am not like Joe, or my husband who is similarly skilled at those gospel comebacks. Instead He wants us to be who we were created to be. And I love to bake.

Struggling to connect with the young people in our youth drop-in centre because I am not exactly 'cool and trendy,' I finally resorted to bribery. Baking a large batch of melt-in-the-mouth cookies, I found my popularity sky-rocketed overnight and I have never forgotten the response of one 16-year-old: certainly the most heartfelt and unusual compliment given to someone in Christian ministry, "These are f***ing brilliant."

On another memorable occasion I created a tray of mini pavlovas for a friend's 80th birthday because his family wanted some gluten-free treats for their dad. They proved so popular that someone eventually resorted to hiding the tray.

That is not to say I have not had food and failure combined (I am the sort of person who is easily distracted with disastrous results) but the point is that for me, God opportunities happen when I am comfortable in my own skin, accepting my weakness and limitations and willing to put what (often little) I have at Jesus' disposal.

This is a posture and heart attitude of humility that does not try to overcomplicate things. It recognises that each of us has unique strengths and weaknesses, and these also create unique opportunities, especially when we consider the spheres of influence in which we live and work.

Events and programmes, organised outreaches and intentional ministry opportunities all have their place and time. But I believe we need to challenge the idea that mission is only about something we schedule (a Kids Club or outreach event) or something reserved for a select few experts or professionals (the evangelists or missionaries).

I have spoken individually here but this principle also applies corporately to small groups or to larger church congregations. Rather than attempting to squeeze ourselves into a particular model of mission or live up to certain expectations, can we get back to the basics of following Jesus and allowing Him to guide our steps as we respond to the opportunities that arise naturally? Can we offer Him who we are and what we have, and allow Him to inspire us with tailor-made solutions?

In the (dare-I-say-it) new normal of post-pandemic Ireland perhaps it is time to re-discover the simplicity and humility of mission as a way of life for everyone, especially the "foolish, the weak, the lowly and the despised..." because we are the ones God chooses.[14]

Humility is foundational because it strips away our reliance on our self and teaches us to follow where Jesus leads. It is also a posture that enables us to listen and respond to our community as we will see in chapter four.

Lord of the Harvest, teach us to follow you with eyes wide open to the opportunities you have prepared for us along the way.

Take Time to Ponder

1. What does it mean to allow God to take the lead? Do we wait on Him for direction?

2. How do we discern what Jesus is saying to us as a church community and not just as individuals? Are we available, like a waiter who keeps a watchful eye on the guest ready to respond as soon as there is a need?

3. When everything is stripped away, what is left? Where have we become reliant on our programmes and structures? How can we simplify our approach to mission?

4. How can we empower each Christian to follow Jesus into everyday life? Do we allow sufficient space for God encounters and happy coincidences? Are we expectant that the Holy Spirit is working in people's lives?

CHAPTER FOUR

Listening

"To answer before listening – that is folly and shame." Proverbs 18:13

In the comedy sci-fi movie, *Galaxy Quest,* a group of has-been actors from a discontinued TV sci-fi show now make a living by appearing at fan conventions and product launches. When members of an alien race watch a recording of the show believing it to be a historical record, they contact the 'crew' of the intergalactic spaceship NSEA Protector to appeal for help.

Commander Peter Quincy Taggart (Tim Allen) agrees to the 'gig' although he is still suffering from a hangover. Assuming they are fanatical fans, he is more interested in the beautiful young alien sitting next to him in the back of the limousine than in the desperate plight of the alien delegation. He has no idea they need him for a rescue mission several light years away.

"You know guys, I had a late night with a Cromorian Fangor Beast so I'm going to shut my eyes for a bit," he tells them. "Go on. I'm listening to everything you say." And promptly falls asleep.

While I am not a great comedy fan, I have always enjoyed this movie. And I have often used the scene to explain how NOT to listen. But I think it also illustrates one of the problems facing followers of Jesus. It is all too easy to make assumptions about our neighbours, work colleagues or friends, about a particular group or the wider community, without taking time to listen and to understand what they are going through. We can close our eyes or look the other way when, like the aliens in the movie, those around us are struggling or suffering. If we are too preoccupied or distracted by our own priorities, prejudices and assumptions, we can miss people's (often silent) cries for help.

Learning to Listen

Listening is one of the greatest gifts we can give, whether as individuals or as church communities.

Helen Locke works as a Counsellor/Psychotherapist at Haven Counselling, Bray and co-leads the Bethel Sozo Ministry in Ireland. She has an MA in Applied Theology and a BSc in Counselling and Psychotherapy. In her VOX magazine article *In Search Of Wholeness,* she wrote this:

> Active listening is a key ingredient of empathy. This type of listening does not interrupt, give advice, make assumptions, judgements or corrections but clarifies by asking questions, attending to body language and feelings, not just words. Real listening requires full concentration, undivided attention and accurate reflection and feedback of what is said.
>
> People sometimes drop "door openers" into conversations to test whether a person is safe to talk to. An attentive ear will respond by asking open ended questions that show concern and interest, allowing the other person to share more deeply, if safe to do so.
>
> The gospels describe many accounts of Jesus listening and engaging with people such as the Samaritan woman at the well[1] and the two disciples on the road to Emmaus.[2]
>
> The Anabaptist author David Augsburger summarised the importance of effective listening when he identified that "being heard is so close to being loved that for the average person, they are almost indistinguishable." This highlights the importance of intentionally teaching some basic listening skills.[3]

If being heard is akin to being loved, then actively listening to individuals, groups or the wider community is a way in which we can demonstrate Christ's love to them.

In his book *Mission-Shaped Evangelism,* Steve Hollinghurst emphasises the importance of listening in the context of mission, especially to avoid preconceived ideas about how to share the message of the gospel. Unless we listen carefully and thoroughly to our culture and our particular context, he says, we will be unable "to stand in the shoes of those [we] seek to communicate with" and we will "end up like the tourists who insist on speaking their own language and simply speak louder and slower if they are not understood."[4]

In the past, barriers of language and culture were considered in cross-cultural mission, but people rarely gave thought to these things within their own country. And yet, in our rapidly changing world, even our own language and culture are changing at an alarming rate. While some constants remain, there has been accelerated change in recent years. The Ireland of the Celtic Tiger felt very different to the Ireland of the recession. Years of austerity then gave way to a slow process of recovery (much slower if, like us, you live outside of Dublin and the major cities). The declining influence of the institutional church was highlighted in the two recent referendums, but there have also been other major shifts in attitudes and the mood of the nation, such as those shaped by Brexit and the rise of far right ideologies.

And of course, the pandemic introduced further changes. A few months ago, if I had talked of "social distancing" no one would have had a clue what I was talking about. Concepts like comorbidities were alien to anyone outside the medical field and Zoom meetings were for the initiated few.

All this means that listening is not just an exercise to be carried out once before moving on to other things. A community survey conducted two years ago is almost certainly out of date today. Deep listening goes beyond hearing what people are saying and it is hard work. It involves both understanding and what psychologists describe as compassionate empathy. It is a continual process that requires humility on the part of the listener. Just as our understanding of God is "through a glass darkly," so our understanding of our communities, our neighbours and even our friends is limited.[5]

Answering Without Listening

Churches all over Ireland have established amazing projects and programmes as they seek to meet the needs of their local community and to share the gospel of Jesus Christ. I have often reported these stories in VOX magazine. But there can also be a tendency to replicate certain projects, especially if they have been successful elsewhere. Even within Ireland one community will differ greatly from another. Inner city Dublin is not the same as the affluent suburbs. Two small towns in rural Ireland can be vastly different depending on history, economics and immigration.

Congregations can feel the pressure to 'do something' to reach out without fully considering what the particular needs or the best approaches are in their community. When this happens, the danger is to answer without listening. Churches may inadvertently duplicate the work of local community groups or create services for which there is no real need in their context. A particular method of sharing the good news of Jesus may be perfect in one setting but a complete disaster in another.

As Fraser Hosford so carefully explained in *Down With This Sort of Thing* we can make the same mistake when it comes to our wider culture. How often do we base our programmes and strategies on research from the UK or America? How often are we reading books or purchasing resources that have been developed for a completely different situation?

Contextualisation involves looking intently; asking questions and listening carefully to the answers we receive, without making up our minds beforehand. If we fail to do this, we will address questions that nobody is asking or seek to meet needs that are not felt.

I love how Jesus shows respect to those who come to Him. Even when the problem seems obvious (the man is blind for goodness sake), Jesus doesn't make assumptions.[6] Instead He asks, "What do you want me to do for you?" This is really important. Jesus gives people the dignity of choice.

In a seminar on Community Transformation at the New Wine Ireland conference (Sligo 2018), Gemma Kelly and Emma Lynch from Tearfund Ireland described the emotions associated with poverty and suffering as "powerlessness, inferiority, hopelessness, depression, isolation and fear."

For many, poverty means being trapped in cycles of shame and humiliation that are more deeply rooted than the physical reality of the lack of money. "When we work in a community, it is not enough for us to say,

'You need water' if we don't first ask them. When we come in and decide what they need rather than consulting them, it reinforces that sense of powerlessness," Gemma Kelly said. Following Jesus' example with the blind man, Tearfund Ireland seeks to listen carefully to overseas communities and involve people in finding solutions for the challenges they face. It is a process that may take more time but it produces long-lasting transformation in individual lives and whole communities.[7]

And what works overseas can offer profound lessons for mission in Ireland. "Go out and listen to people in your community. Hear with fresh ears," Gemma Kelly says.

Our God sees and hears. He responds to the heart cries of His people. He understands our physical needs but He also meets the deepest needs of our heart. So when a paralysed man is lowered to the floor in front of Him, Jesus tells him, "Your sins are forgiven" before He says, "Get up and walk."[8] When the Leper approaches, Jesus breaks the religious and societal norms by touching him - a profound act of acceptance accompanied by the powerful words, "I am willing..."[9]

Whispers and Groans

Two aspects we have discovered that are important to mention are whispers and groans. In Ireland, and most especially in rural Ireland, people will rarely tell you to your face when you have done wrong, or even if they believe, (sometimes mistakenly) that you have done wrong.

Instead, people whisper. And as with any whispers, the truth gradually becomes distorted and the facts are obscured. Rumours spread like wildfire in smaller communities and without allies, it may take months or years before you learn what is being said about you. Even then some people may prefer the rumours to the truth: gossip is more palatable.

How will you react when you are the subject of those whispers? When our listening brings us into contact with painful truths, or even falsehoods about ourselves, it can leave us raw and hurting. And as a Jesus-follower, what will you do when you hear whispers about someone else?

There are also many people who are suffering in our communities whose groans are silenced by fear, shame, stigma and oppression. People find it extremely difficult to ask for help and many will not want to 'burden' anyone with the true narrative of their pain. It takes time, patience, integrity and trustworthiness on the part of the listener before people feel safe to hint at what is going on behind closed doors (perhaps those 'door openers' that Helen Locke mentions).

What a radical gift to our community it would be if followers of Jesus were able to listen to and understand the language of whispers and groans. And how precious it is when we can react with mercy, justice and humility to what we hear.

But what does it look like in practice to begin to listen to individuals and to our wider community? And how can we allow that principle of listening to inform and inspire our mission? Let us look at some examples.

• • •

Listening in the Inner City

Ringsend, Dublin

By Joe Donnelly

"I have indeed seen the oppression of my people in Egypt. I have heard their groaning and have come down to set them free..." Acts 7:34

Often as Christians, we have an expectation that we have a right to be listened to. Where did that come from? I believe it is a product of Christendom but Christendom does not exist any more. At times, we do have those wonderful moments when the Holy Spirit leads us into unique opportunities, but that is a rare privilege.

Jesus listened to people. He allowed them to express their questions, their doubts and their concerns. On the road to Emmaus, He did not announce His resurrection. Instead He came alongside the disciples, asking questions and listening carefully (I would call it 'extravagantly') to their distress.[10]

Listening is the framework for mission. Think about the most epic event of the Old Testament - the Exodus. Before anything happens, God is listening to the cry of His people and He responds by inviting Moses to work with Him to set them free. "I have indeed seen the misery of my people in Egypt. I have heard them crying out because of their slave drivers, and I am concerned about their suffering. So I have come down to rescue them..."[11]

This is a constant theme throughout scripture. God is looking for listeners - those who will hear the word of the Lord but also heed the cries of the people.

Listening is one of my key principles in mission and has led to a number of projects for us in Ringsend. We start by engaging in an intentional strategy of listening and then, having listened, we go back to God and tell Him what we are hearing. God is hearing it already but He wants us to hear it too, and to work with Him to set people free.

Studying for my Masters Degree at the Irish Bible Institute accelerated this for me: it was transformational in my life and ministry, especially the lessons about different types of listening. Now, when somebody comes and says, "Joe, can I see you about a few flowers?" (and it happens quite often), I can tell from their body language when their problem has nothing to do with flowers. Usually, within a few minutes, I will find an opportunity to pray with them about whatever is really bothering them.

At the Anchorage Project, we began a discreet and informal process of listening to those over 55 years of age about the subject of loneliness. For about two years, we kept asking two questions – what do you think most people might consider to be the loneliest time of the day and what might most people consider to be the loneliest day of the week?

The rough outline of what we were hearing could be summarised as follows, "I suppose that the loneliest time of the day is between 6pm and 9pm, and the toughest day of the week is Wednesday because social welfare payments are paid on Thursday morning."

At a local community awards event, I fell into conversation with the Lord Mayor of Dublin. He told me that his mother would call him at the same time every evening, around six or seven o'clock because she felt lonely.

Although there are many agencies providing affordable dinners for people at lunchtime, nothing much was happening during the evening to help these people. We began to pray, and then we started to see if doors would open for a gospel-shaped response.

We decided that we would do a weekly meal, each Wednesday, from 7:00pm – 8:30pm. Everyone would work as volunteers to provide a first class three-course meal and the Anchorage Project would cover the wholesale cost of the food. We would charge each diner €5 for attending and this €5 would go into a separate community support fund to help needy causes in the locality.

When the doors opened, we were shocked to see a crowd of people queuing up in the cold weather to come inside. Some were using Zimmer frames, and chairs were moved around to get someone in who was in a wheelchair. Another person needed help because he had an oxygen bottle with him while someone else suffered with early onset Alzheimer's and also needed watching.

When everyone finished their meal, we explained about the story of the loaves and the fishes. We told them that we would collect five euro from each person if they could afford it and when we reached the sum of €1,000 we would ask our diners what they thought we should do with the money.

We wanted them to tell us if they heard of someone whose home had been broken into, or someone who had been recently bereaved or hospitalised and we would use this money to support and encourage them.

In due course, our five euro fund reached the €1,000 mark and I asked our diners what they thought we should do with this significant sum of money. We had heard the news that the local under-12 girl's soccer team had just qualified for the cup final. However, their lock up facility had been broken into and their equipment was either destroyed or stolen. We said, if it was okay with everyone present, we would approach the manager of the girl's team and ask them to get a quotation for replacing what was stolen.

Eventually, we were able to replace everything with brand new equipment that the wholesaler gave at trade price when he heard who was paying. This gesture provided the girls with a huge encouragement in their cup final. They beat the team who were runaway favourites and brought their trophy into the café the following Wednesday evening to loud cheers from all of our diners.

Asking Questions

We started a Community Volunteer Network that meets once a month for a complimentary breakfast. In order to qualify for the 'free breakfast' each volunteer must be willing to do a minimum of four hours voluntary work. Each month a different community leader (political, religious, sporting, journalism, youth, mental health, etc.) is invited to participate in the breakfast and answer five key questions:

1. Tell us about yourself.
2. Tell us about what you do in the community.
3. Tell us about your hopes for the community.
4. Tell us about your fears for the community.
5. Tell us about a local project that needs volunteer help.

After breakfast, we select a local project as the focus for the follow-up volunteer session. Success largely depends upon establishing clear communication with the project leader as well as proper preparation and organisation.

Around two months after completing the volunteer task, we contact the project leader and tell him or her that we would like to use our weekly prayer meeting to pray for their project. We offer to phone them back later to ask for some specific points that we can pray about and where appropriate, ask them if they would allow us to use a room at their premises for our prayer meeting.

If the project leader is resistant to our prayer meeting idea, we approach the community leader who originally answered questions at the breakfast. We extend to them the same offer of prayer.

Discussing the prospect of holding a prayer meeting with a 'secular' community leader where they are the entire focus of the meeting is something that is refreshingly and deeply challenging, especially when you have already blessed them by performing a volunteer work project.

This discussion will usually involve explaining what prayer is, how it works and why we believe in it. The offer of phoning back later to get their specific prayer points has often allowed a lively and profound discussion to take place at an inner city community project around the subject of prayer needs. On occasions, some of the staff have shown up on the night of our prayer meeting and asked specifically for prayer for themselves.

Conversations in the Garden

Developing an urban garden space that is exploding with flowers and singing canaries throughout the summer months has been part of the ministry in Ringsend for many years. The flowers create beauty and sales from the plants raise funds for vital projects both in Ireland and overseas. But the garden has also given rise to many conversations that have demonstrated the need to listen carefully and prayerfully to those who visit.

When Marie visited our garden one summer lunchtime, she was amazed by our flowers. I explained that the inspiration behind our garden came from our first parents, who lived in a beautiful garden where they could experience the presence of God. Marie bluntly replied that she was a complete unbeliever in any sort of a God.

Suspecting that there was a big story behind Marie's response, I gave her a trailing begonia and asked her to take it back to her own little garden and nurture it. Marie was delighted with my offer and accepted the plant.

Marie was soon back and wanted some more ideas for her garden. As I shared some tips with her, I found it easy to bring up the subject of having faith in God. Marie said that she was a survivor of the infamous Magdalene Laundries. When I heard this, I immediately understood why she was sharp in her comments about God.

Against the backdrop of our lovely flowers, our canaries singing, the sound of preschool children playing, as well as the aroma of fresh food cooking in our café, I was conscious of the Lord leading Marie into this space to minister His healing touch into her brokenness and pain. I decided to wait until she returned for another visit before speaking, as I wanted to pray into this matter.

Within a few days, Marie was back again and continued to be dismissive with her references about God. After answering her initial questions about flowers, I took a leap of faith and said, "You may feel that God was responsible for the abuse that you suffered but I can most definitely tell you that He was not. Successive political and religious leaders established and perpetuated that institution where you suffered. Those political and religious leaders were responsible for its operations. If you insist on blaming God for what happened to you at the hands of the Magdalene Laundries then you would be doing God a serious injustice. If you read the gospel accounts you will see that the Lord Jesus Himself suffered horrific abuse at the hands of the political and religious leaders of His day."

Marie listened respectfully to my comments and then headed off with her flowers without saying much. We prayed that Marie would come back soon for a visit and sure enough, within a few days, she came back again for more flowers. This time around, she seemed to have a different tone and attitude.

When I commented on the weather she replied, "It's a beautiful day, thank God." Although it was just a simple comment, I was encouraged at Marie's positive and quite pointed reference to God. This positivity continued throughout our conversation and I was delighted when Marie said that, despite poor literacy levels, she had begun reading the gospels to discover more about this Jesus who suffered such abuse at the hands of political and religious leaders.

Marie has continued to make slow progress in her journey into a healing experience with Jesus Christ. We are praying that she will experience the 'beauty for ashes" that the Lord Jesus promises to those who seek Him.

• • •

Double Listening

Ballina

By Marian Edwards and Emma Bolster Rodrigues

Jesus spent 30 years listening and only three years in ministry. He listened to the people He would later serve.[12] This is what we did in Ballina. We spent time listening to the people living in our community to find out about the needs. The exploratory stage was a time of discovery. It was a process of discerning as we looked for signs of where the Holy Spirit was working and sought to build relationships with individuals, families and groups.

Listening inevitably leads to prayer because, as Jesus-followers, we cannot hear the heart cries of our community and remain unmoved. Jesus had compassion on the crowds because they were "sheep without a shepherd."[13]

Hollinghurst calls this double listening - listening to the culture and listening to what the Scriptures have to say in response. "Theologically, the importance of double listening flows from a belief that God is at work in all cultures and all people."[14]

Creating a Place of Peace

One thing we learnt was that there was a lack of facilities for people to meet and chat. There were cafés but teenagers were not allowed in and the Traveller community often felt stigmatised. There was a need to create a space where people could feel accepted and listened to. In *The Viral Gospel,* Alex Absalom describes this as a "place of peace."[15]

The Big Blue Bus became that safe space. In 2018, Emma discovered an old library bus on Done Deal and the churches raised the funds to buy it. The Ballina Churches Together in partnership with Church Army, fitted out the bus as a mobile drop-in centre.

A group of men would come onto the bus on Saturday and Sunday nights. These men live alone; they are vulnerable and isolated. They enjoyed the sense of community and looked forward to it each week. We parked in the centre of the town at Tesco's car park and the men would come on board for a cup of tea and a good conversation rather than going to a pub.

Many felt we listened to them and cared about them, even when it seemed that no one else did. These men are on the fringes of society and many do not have families around them. The Big Blue Bus provides a space for community, where they can meet and feel both welcomed and accepted. We listen, chat, laugh, sing and pray with them. They have become our friends.

Every weekend, many young people throng the streets of Ballina. The Big Blue Bus provides a safe place for them to come and hang out. Many teenagers are facing challenges growing up and struggling with low self-esteem, education and concerns for the future. Some lack basic life-skills, others are facing relationship issues and simply want someone to talk to. A number are from the Traveller community and face additional stigma and abuse as a result. With the teens there is never a dull moment.

• • •

Embracing Listening

As we have seen in the stories from Joe, Marian and Emma, when individuals and churches begin to listen, prayerfully and compassionately, this reveals deeper issues within our communities and inspires missional responses that are appropriately contextualised.

I was struck by the way one church in County Wicklow also found a way forward by listening to the community. When Nigerian-born Solomon Aroboto and his Irish wife Tricia moved into Arklow, they had a passion to do something for God but at the time there were very few black people in the town and locals were sceptical of anything outside their experience. Establishing a church began with prayer and developing relationships with local people. "We spent a lot of time getting to know people over cups of coffee," Solomon said. "Unless people see Jesus in you, they do not care about the Jesus you talk about."

A prayer group eventually grew into a small fellowship but the real breakthrough came when Solomon and Tricia began to notice some of the different groups that were active in the town.

"That was the beginning of a major shift for us. We invited groups like Meals on Wheels, the lifeboat volunteers, the Men's Shed, the local cancer support group and Suicide or Survive to come and visit our church," Solomon explained. "We told them, 'We know that you are doing a good job. Come and tell us about your work. We will pray for you and give you a donation.'"

Some groups seemed reluctant at first, wondering whether there were strings attached, but this attitude changed when they realised the church had no expectations and simply wanted to bless them. It has been a wonderful opportunity for church members to hear first-hand what is happening in the town and to support the work on the ground.

"Once a month, we hold a special service and one of the groups comes to talk about their work. We then present them with a cheque. Over the last six years, we have been able to do that 60 times and the church members have really taken hold of the vision. We are learning about our community and also communicating that we are here to stay and we want to be a blessing. We have become known as a church that helps people. People saw our hearts through our actions and began to feel comfortable with us," Solomon added.

Andrew and I have had to learn this principle of listening the hard way and we still get it wrong. We have often been the fools who rushed in, acting without reflection and taking the knee-jerk approach.

I still remember a time when Andrew was involved in a summer outreach programme alongside various churches in the Midlands. As one of the senior leaders, he had been training others in how to share their faith. Some of the trainees watched in awe as he effortlessly engaged a stranger in conversation and began to talk about Jesus.

When the trainees started to praise him afterwards, Andrew cut them off. "Do you know why I failed?" he asked them. "I did not even ask that man's name."

In a relational culture where who you know is still far more important than what you know, sharing the life-changing message of Jesus without any attempt to understand and relate to the person we are talking to is like that tourist who shouts all the more loudly in a vain attempt to be understood.

Other experiences have given us a glimpse of what is possible when we listen closely to our community and respond in the right way.

The first occurred in 2012 when a number of different community groups in Buncrana began expressing a need for premises. There was very little community space that was not commercially operated or fully booked.

Being part of these groups, we heard the same needs being repeated and so we talked quietly to each of the groups to suggest a more joined-up approach. We facilitated a quick Survey Monkey questionnaire to establish some of the felt needs. The results were remarkably similar.

Organising a meeting over coffees in our local hotel was the start of a journey that resulted in the formation of a charity. Together we set up and began to run a community centre and social enterprise. While at times challenging, the process has given us a rich and deep understanding of the needs of our community and the great privilege of working alongside inspirational community leaders.

On a visit in 2014, President Michael D Higgins said, "The activities of the six member groups who founded [the centre] constitute a vision of human flourishing that goes beyond the provision of basic needs. It is wonderful to see local community groups come together and share their rich experience under the same roof."

A new lesson for us was born out of a painful season of misunderstandings and strained relationships. Approaching the 300th anniversary of our town as it stands today (there has been a settlement here for more than 500 years), we began chatting with a local historian who was keen to mark this milestone.

We joined the discussion enthusiastically and shared ideas about possible events and programmes. We were careful to avoid using the terminology of celebration, having learnt early on that the modern town was built as a result of land-grabbing and evictions by greedy English landlords.

Yet in our naivety and ignorance, we had failed to grasp the depth of wounds caused by centuries of oppression and injustice here. The resulting anger and backlash, albeit from only certain sectors of our community, was too great to accommodate our well-meaning involvement. We did a lot of soul-searching as we stepped back from trying to 'help' in what had become such a contentious issue.

Five years previously, on that visit to the town, Michael D Higgins had quoted, "*Ní neart go cur le chéile* - There is no strength without unity."

Reflecting on the wounds and divisions that had been revealed by the up-coming anniversary, we developed the idea of hosting a meal for local influencers in all sectors of our community. The meal - called *Le Chéile* - would be an opportunity for leaders to share their vision for the future and highlight the sort of town we want to create together.

Of course, there would be food involved too - we wanted to bless and serve our community with a delicious three-course home-cooked meal complete with live entertainment and wonderful company around dinner tables that were beautifully decorated with fresh flowers.

So we sent out the invitations in some degree of trepidation. On the night, over 40 people gathered representing politics, business, education and the community voluntary sector as well as local church leaders. Instead of marking the painful 300th anniversary, the event helped to celebrate the fifth anniversary of our community centre.

Five speakers - the chairperson of the community centre, a politician, a business leader, a young person and a retired secondary school teacher - each shared powerfully and poignantly about the challenges and opportunities we face together as a town.

It was a beautiful evening and an opportunity for us to both serve and listen to our community. Instead of imposing an event that would remind people of pain and injustice, we were able to invite people to enjoy a meal together and to share their heart and their hopes for our town.

Listening is an act of love that demonstrates respect and affirms the value of each person. And as we join God in hearing the cries of people's hearts, He invites us to join Him in His rescue plan.

Oh, for a church that is quick to listen, slow to speak and slow to become angry.

Loving Father, you heard our cry and rescued us. Teach us to listen to those around us and to obey the prompting of your Holy Spirit in response.

Take Time to Ponder

1. Have there been times when you have answered without listening, either individually or as a church? Are we guilty of listening to respond rather than listening to understand? How much does our agenda colour what we hear?

2. Have you experienced good examples of how listening has empowered missional opportunities?

3. How can you find out about the needs in your community? Who are the people you need to talk to? What questions should you ask?

4. If listening is akin to love how are we intentional about listening? What happens when we hear something negative or critical?

5. Where are the places where people are having conversations? Do you go there? Are you willing just to listen? This could be a physical space or an online forum. If there are no safe places for conversation or discussion, can you initiate one?

CHAPTER FIVE

Hospitality

"You give them something to eat." Luke 9:13

As veteran travellers, we have been welcomed into the homes and hearts of friends and strangers all over the world. And while I am reluctant to spill too many beans, among the beautiful memories of generous hosts and delicious meals, we have had our fair share of more 'interesting' experiences.

Like the time we arrived back to where we were staying late at night, after everyone else had retired, only to discover someone had forgotten to put out any bedding for the sofa bed. We had to improvise bed coverings from the clothes we had with us but were too cold to get much sleep.

Or the time when a generous career woman allowed us to stay in her flat (with our toddler) for a week. Our attempts to toddler-proof the lovely home, lifting fragile ornaments out of the way, were thwarted when each day she would call in and return everything to its original place.

The worst for me happened in Spain. After driving for ten hours in 40-degree heat without air conditioning, we finally reached our accommodation only to see a large cockroach scuttling across the floor. I confess to a major meltdown.

Open Hearts

You do not have to go far in Ireland to come across the familiar phrase, Céad míle fáilte - even our tourist board (Fáilte Ireland) is named after the world-famous Irish welcome. Of course, we know reality can fall far short of the rosy stereotype, but as we unpack what mission in Ireland looks like in practice, openhearted hospitality is one of the hallmarks. It is a foundational posture that is deeply ingrained in the Irish psyche.

In ancient Ireland, the duty of hospitality was enshrined in Brehon Law. Welcoming and feeding visitors (the root word is 'stranger') was not just an ideal, it was a legal obligation for homeowners and especially for the *Rí* - the king. Irish legends and historical fiction feature the wealthy *briugu* or in modern Irish *brughaidh* (translated hospitaller) who owned guesthouses at busy crossroads and offered hospitality to all travellers. They were required by law to be ready to welcome, accommodate and feed guests at all times.

To this was added the understanding that to welcome a guest was to welcome Christ. "Since every guest is Christ – no trifling saying – better is humility, better gentleness, better liberality towards him."[1]

In 1584, English traveller Richard Stanihurst wrote of the Irish chieftains, "They have fixed manors and habitations, which are daily filled with a great throng of guests. They are without doubt the most hospitable of men, nor could you please them more in anything than by frequently visiting their houses..."[2]

In New Testament times, Paul identifies hospitality (the Greek word means 'lover of strangers') as one of the defining characteristics of Christian leaders[3] while Peter calls believers to show 'ungrudging' hospitality towards one another.[4]

And the writer to the Hebrews suggests Christians have entertained angels unawares, by showing hospitality to strangers.

Hospitality given and received was at the centre of Jesus' ministry. He ate meals with tax collectors and 'sinners.' He fed the 5,000 and the 4,000. He was a guest in the homes of friends (Martha and Mary) and of the not so welcoming (Simon the Pharisee). He shared the Passover Meal with His disciples. He broke bread with the disciples on the road to Emmaus and served breakfast on the beach for the returning fishermen in John 21.

When He gave, Jesus did so with outrageous generosity: there were

12 basket-loads of leftovers from the feeding of the 5,000 and His contribution to the wedding at Cana seems extravagant.

In the early church, hospitality and ministry went hand in hand. Acts 2:46 says, "They broke bread in their homes and ate together with glad and sincere hearts." The believers were dispersed and scattered throughout the community (like yeast in the dough). Acts 5:42 adds, "Day after day, in the temple courts and from house to house, they never stopped teaching and proclaiming the good news that Jesus is the Messiah."

In *Dine with Me,* Amos Yong writes, "Christian mission is nothing more or less than our participation in the hospitality of God. God is not only the principal 'missionary' but also the host of all creation who invites the world to 'God's banquet of salvation.' Evangelisation is... nothing more or less than our having experienced God's redemptive hospitality and our inviting others to experience the same."[5]

As with "presence," this principle is focused around sharing our lives with people and is characterised by generosity of spirit, especially towards those that the rest of society fails to welcome and embrace - the strangers or the outcasts. When Paul was shipwrecked on the island of Malta, he encountered "unusual kindness."[6] If it is God's kindness that leads us to repentance, can our acts of kindness and hospitality bring about a similar response?[7]

Hospitality and food are recurring themes for my co-authors and in many other ministries I have encountered around Ireland.

The wonderful thing about the Kingdom of Heaven is that sometimes the ones who appear to have the least, are able to give the most. Those extending lavish hospitality and outrageous generosity are not restrained or constrained by the lack of resources. They offer what they have and allow Jesus to multiply.

This is where the limitation of the small, the weak and the under-resourced is turned into strength. Rather than arriving as the powerful, rich and influential rescuers into our community, can we follow Jesus in receiving and, at times, requesting hospitality (He asked the Samaritan woman for a drink)? A new dynamic emerges when we are vulnerable and willing to ask for help. Humbled by our insufficiency, this Christ-like descent opens the possibility for new and enriched relationships.

• • •

Ministering the Love of God

Ringsend, Dublin

By Joe Donnelly

Developing the Fair Play Café as a place of welcome and hospitality for the community in Ringsend was just the beginning for us. It also created an opportunity to minister the love of God to those who were in need.

In Mark 6:5-44, there is a familiar story of the disciples coming to Jesus with a problem. Thousands of people have nothing to eat. Jesus' response to His disciples was quite alarming, "You give them something to eat."

After doing the sums, His disciples claimed that it would take up to half a year's wages to feed the people. The strange thing is that Jesus did not ask His disciples to "feed the people," He simply told them to "give them something to eat." Jesus was deliberately challenging His disciples to take whatever they had and simply place it into His hands.

We began praying about the issue of local food poverty. Our plan was to be able to give people a hearty lunch in our café completely free of charge. Using Mark 6 as our template, we considered what we had that God might use as a catalyst. We realised that, if we put a tips jar on our counter beside our till and if our customers would put approximately €50 per week in loose change into the jar, this then could be our equivalent of five loaves and two fishes.

We estimated we could raise approximately €200 - €250 each month from our tips jar. We could then invite a company, group or individual to match that amount and so our €200 could become €400 each month.

We decided to develop a type of "loyalty" card, similar to those used by supermarkets. Each of these cards would have €10 credit and we could distribute them to community police, home school liaison teachers, local St. Vincent De Paul volunteers, etc. This meant that approximately 40 local people could come to us each month and enjoy lunch completely free of charge. The loyalty card for the initiative was to be identical to that used by regular customers of the Fair Play Café, so there could be no distinction or shame in using the scheme.

When we started the initiative to match our €200 in tips, the first person to step forward was a local woman in her late 80s whose daughter had lived and died on Dublin's streets as a homeless rough sleeper. This old lady gave us €1,000. We named this initiative 'Share your Lunch' after the boy in John 6:9.

When 14-year-old Aiden first came into our café, he was holding one of our €10 loyalty cards. Like so many people in his position, Aiden awkwardly approached our café counter and nervously asked for some food. Within minutes, he left the café with as much food as he could carry and a few days later, he was back again for more.

Aiden and his mum Carol live in a nearby cottage, which we later discovered was without electricity or basic services. After lots of enquiries, I discovered that they are believed to be part of a witness protection programme and are hiding out in their cottage while fearing for their lives. Aiden's mum Carol does not want to have contact with anyone. Aiden must go to school each day and so, he comes into our café to get food for himself and his mother. Getting healthy food to a family like this is only an initial step in the outreach of God's love towards this family.

Carol refused to open the door when we knocked and never replied to several notes that we posted through her letterbox. Our next step was to talk again to local charity groups, schools, clergy, health board and mental health officials who had known about Aiden's case for years and had reached a stalemate with the family.

We then decided to create a part-time paid holiday job for Aiden. This work would include watering our flowers, cleaning out our rabbit hutches and canary cages as well as sweeping and cleaning outdoor areas. This has been a massive positive development for Aiden as it has provided some work each week during the school holidays along with food for his Mum and himself.

It has been amazing to see Aiden carefully sowing herbs, flowers and vegetables. Slowly but surely the realisation strikes you that perhaps this is a way that our Father wants His kingdom to come to this family at this stage in their journey.

Rehabilitation of Hope

"...the Lord has anointed me to proclaim good news to the poor." Isaiah 61:3

Another example came in the lead up to Christmas as we looked for opportunities to present God's upside down kingdom in a fresh and unexpected way. We extended invitations to victims of domestic violence from the local accommodation centre.

We sectioned off an area of our café with posh tablecloths, cutlery, fresh flowers and table decorations. As this was something that our regular customers seldom see, it caused quite a stir. Curiosity was rife concerning the identity of these important guests. We explained that we were hosting a special group of VIPs but that the whole thing was a 'hush hush' event.

As we expected, word started spreading in local offices, schools and workplaces that some big name celebs were going to be showing up at our café. The following day these same regulars were shocked to see that women from the local centre for the victims of domestic violence were occupying the tables. After the meal, we presented each mum with a hamper of chocolates, flowers and perfume as well as a small present for their children.

This initiative provided an interpretation of the Christmas story, where victims of domestic violence as well as patrons of a busy lunchtime café, see the upside down kingdom expressed as good news to the poor.

Subsequent 'follow-up' events took place throughout the summer for these VIPs, including a 'ready, steady, plant' session where each guest learned how to plant up a hanging basket and then took the basket back to their flat.

Breakfast Invitation

At another time, hosting a Teddy Bear's Breakfast for pre-school children was a way to support a number of families under stress. The children could wear dressing gowns, PJs and slippers and bring their favourite teddy bear. And they could invite up to three other members of their family.

The parents would provide a sheet of paper with the child's ideal breakfast and we would do our best to provide this, while other family members would have a standard breakfast. The event took place on a weekend in early June, with breakfast provided free of charge although voluntary contributions could be accepted for a designated charity.

Examples of how an event like this can have far reaching consequences become clear when you receive feedback.

Three-and-a-half year old Conor was not happy when his mum told him that she was inviting her parents as guests to accompany them to his Teddy Bear's Breakfast. Conor's mum and dad were splitting up and he wasn't happy that his dad was being excluded from his special breakfast. Conor insisted that his dad should be invited along with his mum and his teddy. Although his mum tried every means to persuade him to change his mind, Conor was not prepared to exclude his dad.

When the breakfast took place, it was great to see Conor and his teddy sitting with his mum and dad as they all enjoyed the breakfast together. Within a few weeks of the event, we heard that Conor's parents were considering staying together and giving their marriage another chance.

• • •

Loaves and Fishes Café

Arklow

By Robert Holden

For 15 years we had been asking, "How does a small non-denominational church in a medium-sized Irish town get involved in its community?" Our congregation - Bridge Christian Community - was mostly made up of blow-ins and people who did not live in the town, so finding ways to get alongside people, outside of personal contacts, seemed elusive. We secured a lease on a property in town during 2010 and made the building available as a community centre during the week, but in terms of the church serving the community, it remained a resource of huge untapped potential. We believed God wanted the venue to be a lampstand for the light of the church to be seen.

A series of light bulb moments started sparking in 2013. At a leaders' conference, I heard a talk by Noel Kenny of Liberty Church, Dublin about establishing a 'perma-reach' into the community. Inspired by the rebuilding of Jerusalem's walls recorded in Nehemiah 3, he took the names of two of the city gates to describe different aspects of the church's mission.

The Sheep Gate symbolised the activities and structures needed to look after church members, while the Fish Gate signified finding ways of constantly reaching out to not-yet believers.

Following this, two visits to Arklow from seasoned missionaries and church-planters also left their mark.

One couple said they had dared to ask: "If our church disappeared tomorrow, would anybody miss it?" That had led them to go beyond worship and teaching, to establish a community house and series of serving opportunities in their area in Northern Ireland. They said that often it felt like keeping people alive long enough to give them the chance to respond to Jesus.

The others, arriving in a new context to plant a church in the Pacific, found they could not break into the parts of the community they were targeting. They felt God say: "You look after the people I give you and I will look after the rest." That opened their eyes to the most disadvantaged around them, and they set up ministries among the poor, sex workers and people with learning difficulties.

With these examples ringing in our ears, we continued to pray about what this could mean for us. The answer that came back, unexpectedly, was 'food', but we did not know what it meant or what to do with it.

Chatting in a local shop, I discovered someone with chef training who wanted to cook for people who really needed it. This idea started to germinate. Shortly afterwards, a group of teenagers from the church travelled to the UK for a mission trip where they spent an afternoon at an allotment growing vegetables for a city homeless service. Two other unrelated conversations that same day brought up the topic of feeding people and on the last night of the trip, the group was invited to an evening of worship and prophetic prayer.

After speaking into the lives of each of the young people, someone started praying with me, saying: "I see you feeding people." At this point I laughed – God really seemed to want to get through. Then the person prophesying continued saying that the church would be linked up with supermarkets wanting to give away food. I took that as the sign of someone getting carried away, embellishing what God had shown them. But I had to swallow my scepticism on arriving home and opening my emails. There were two announcing the launch of Food Cloud, an organisation specifically aimed at connecting supermarkets and suppliers to charities who could use surplus food.

At the same time, a local councillor had encountered a number of temporarily homeless young people camping out in parts of the town. The church knew it was time to act.

What to do, though? A team formed to take the action forward. Initially, we considered a soup and sandwich run for those sleeping rough but somehow that did not sit right. We looked at what we had: a heart to serve, a building in the town centre with a large kitchen and people who were not afraid of cooking in large quantities.

These were the 'loaves and fishes' that we wanted to give to Jesus to multiply. We decided simply to cook a meal and see if anyone would come, beginning with 25 portions and virtually no publicity, as we wanted to test-drive the process. Within a few weeks, word had got around town and we were serving 50 portions, offering takeaways as well as sit-down meals at the weekly café.

Early in the New Year, the numbers jumped to 80 and continued to grow. The church connected with Food Cloud and collected surplus stock from a local supermarket, keeping the meat for the Tuesday meals and distributing the rest to households.

"Serving the love of Jesus on a plate" was the way one church member described the service and what struck the team from the beginning was that food was only the vehicle for a lot more to be given. Many of the first people to come in lived alone and were delighted to have a place to go to find company. There was a policy of 'no questions asked, no strings attached' so people only shared their situations if they chose to, but companionship proved to be one of the key hungers.

The simple act of kindness struck people at the heart level too, with several saying that they were not used to experiencing that. Families found a place to come and feel welcomed, as did people with no stable homes, some with addiction or mental health challenges and some with learning difficulties.

Teenagers came after school to study and get some food. Church members found a place where they could spend time together outside of a meeting context. And for a small church that for 15 years had not felt they had really connected with the local community, suddenly there was a Tuesday congregation of people from all parts of the town, all walks of life, and the wider community could grasp and get behind what was going on.

Offers of help and donations started to come in from other churches, from local businesses and individuals. There may have been an element of misunderstanding in this – people often saw it as a 'soup kitchen for the homeless' though this has never been the reality and the church has never communicated about Loaves and Fishes Café in that way.

However, a lamp had been lit and set on a stand, a lamp that has now burned for over five and a half years, with most of the finances coming from donations or two main fundraising events per year.

What, then, is the nature of this ministry? The key elements are simplicity, mercy and community. Would the people who come in starve without it? Probably not, though we know that for some it is their only or main source of nutritious food. Do some regulars use it as a way of saving money for other, less healthy spending? Undoubtedly. But the team holds on to the vision that by showing mercy without any form of judgement, they are showing Christ. Which one of us deserves His grace and provision?

And by sitting at the tables week by week and offering a listening ear, they have had many opportunities to pray with people, to encourage and sometimes to get involved in other ways. There have been a few instances where people say they would not be alive today without the help of Loaves and Fishes Café.

Has it led to many people turning to Jesus and being added to the church? No, at least not in the sense of Sunday attendance but that is never the goal of kingdom mission. There have been some who have come on Sundays and who have clearly had experiences of God's goodness, but few have 'stuck' in terms of regular involvement.

But if the flock entrusted to our care is the community and the church just the sheepfold, then the church is now caring for far more than it would be without Loaves and Fishes Café, and is having a 'perma-reach' into the area.

Serving Together

Nowhere is this seen more clearly than in the bank of volunteers. While the core team is made up of people from the church, the opportunity to serve is open to anyone who wants to, subject to an application process. The main stipulation is that they take time to sit down with the guests at some point so that there is no sense of 'us and them.'

There have been well over 100 different people registered as volunteers, with around 30 serving at any one time and 15 needed on any given week. From retired business owners to ex-offenders, Transition Year and foreign exchange students, from those in post-addiction programmes to chefs, the team has been as diverse as the guests. The church culture places a high value on serving and this has been extended to many others who find fulfilment and fellowship from being part of the team.

Some are involved in other churches, giving a rare sense of co-operation on a practical level, while others have no faith background but are welcomed in and invited to join the weekly prayer time if they wish to. The need for people to give to others is seen most clearly on Christmas Day, when Loaves and Fishes Café throws a party with all the trimmings.

Every year when the booking is opened, it is volunteers who start to fill up the places – people who want somewhere to be and to have something to do on what can be a difficult day for many. Volunteers have found healing and restoration for themselves as they have served others. Truly it is blessed to give as well as receive.

During the Covid-19 restrictions, the café had to confine itself to takeaways and deliveries only, with a limited volunteer team. This totally changed the dynamic, leaving much less room for relationship building. While it was good to be able to maintain the food distribution, it felt like the major part of the ministry had been cut off.

The Loaves and Fishes café has enabled the Bridge Christian Community to punch well above its weight in terms of the number of people impacted from a small core. It is not perfect and probably still has huge areas of untapped potential, but in giving what we have and being careful not to overreach, we have kept a simple and tangible lamp burning for people to see the light of Jesus.

• • •

Embracing Hospitality

As we have seen in the stories from Ringsend and Arklow, hospitality provides opportunities for loving service. It overlaps with each of the other principles we have shared, enabling us to spend time with people, to listen to them, to demonstrate mercy and to respond to the prompting of the Holy Spirit.

While I believe hospitality is an important principle for mission in any part of the world, here in Ireland openhearted hospitality is essential. But that does not mean it has to be complicated. My grandma, who was famed for her open home even through the leanest of times, would quote the story of Mary and Martha with a twist. "Only one thing is needed," she would say, "keep it simple."[8] Jesus affirms the importance of sharing "even a cup of water."[9]

Marian Edwards talks of the 'ministry of smiles' and of generosity. That is a great place to start. Smile at people and see what happens.

The wonderful thing about hospitality is that it allows for creative approaches and a lot of fun. A friend I know loves to bake muffins. She divides them up into greaseproof-wrapped parcels (just two muffins in each parcel) and then takes them with her as she goes to visit neighbours. This simple, loving gesture opens doors and builds relationships.

New Ground Ireland is a ministry with a vision to establish missional communities across Ireland.[10] Hospitality plays a central role in their work in Longford. Founder John Oliver explained, "Our focus is to bring people on a journey. We have simplified everything. There is much less focus on structures, buildings and bank accounts for local groups, just a heart to meet people where they are and see them become disciples of Jesus.

"We began with prayer and a time of worship in the centre of Longford town. Within a few months, we had made connections with people. We started informal home groups - meeting around a meal to share the word of God and break bread together. Those times have been beautiful. The first time we broke bread together at the dinner table someone shouted out, "Communion bread tastes better when you dip it in pepper sauce."

"When several home groups become established we then meet together in the local theatre for worship and celebration. But the focus is not on the central 'hub' or gathering, it is on the small groups. They will be working hard to connect with their neighbours, holding BBQs and seeking to bring them into a faith journey as well. The key is to empower people for mission within their existing networks - their friendship groups (relational), their neighbourhood (locational) and their workplace (vocational)."

Biblical hospitality has this type of outward focus. It is not about showing off - like an episode of *Come Dine with Me* - or attempting to gain favours by entertaining influential people. It is about welcoming people into our lives and sharing what we have with those around us.

Jesus said, "...when you give a banquet, invite the poor, the crippled, the lame, the blind, and you will be blessed. Although they cannot repay you, you will be repaid at the resurrection of the righteous."[11]

Perhaps it is time to review our guest list. Who are the ones that are being overlooked, excluded or rejected by the community? Who are the voiceless? The unloved? Radical hospitality will embrace those that others despise.

For us, running creative arts workshops for clients from the local centre for adults with learning and intellectual disabilities has been humbling and enriching. It opened our eyes to a whole group of people within our community who are often excluded even from our churches. We gained so much from their example of generous welcome and caring concern for one another and for us. And we learnt powerful lessons about the way God reveals Himself to the "least of these."[12] One of the clients was moved to tears when I read from Isaiah 9 at a joint Christmas service and another, who is unable to speak, began to hum *Amazing Grace* when she heard they were coming to do a workshop with us (as part of our annual Amazing Grace Festival).

In her VOX article *Learning Disability and the Church* (Oct 2018) Donna Jennings wrote, "The church leans towards strength, power and knowledge and while there is a place for that, this imitates the values of the world. We need a biblical understanding of the kingdom of God in valuing and including those that the world deems 'worthless.' Often the church can have the same mentality."

If biblical hospitality means having a love for strangers, then we need to ask who are the strangers in our midst? Do we have an openhearted response to those who move into our communities from outside of Ireland - migrants, refugees, asylum seekers, those in direct provision and those who have arrived to work in factories or farms?

Thankfully more churches are waking up to the needs of our new Irish communities but welcome for migrants is often seen as an add-on, the province of a few rather than a core focus of the body of Christ. And it is costly, too. When we start to see 'the Syrians' or 'the Polish' as real people with faces and names, a shift starts to happen. We will no longer be able to tolerate the living conditions of direct provision or the casual racism that is so widespread that most white Irish people do not even notice. And some deny it exists at all.

Even listing some of these different groups and individuals can cause anxiety to start to rise. Our highly programmed lives (or at least those pre-pandemic) allow little space for anything extra. And that is the problem. When the focus of our time and attention is on a series of events, however meaningful, we struggle to be present even to our families, let alone those in our wider community.

In our individualistic society, time is a precious commodity. We tend to compartmentalise and allocate portions of time to different activities - whether it is work, family, leisure or church. A posture of hospitality reorders our priorities to welcome and include people into our lives, journeying together with others rather than making 'appointments' and arranging meetings.

The stay-at-home of lockdown allowed many to reconnect with their own family and neighbourhood. I am sure we were not the only ones to take time to chat with neighbours over the garden fence or those we met during our daily walks.

Hospitality shifted and became more intentional as we reached out and connected to one another using different technologies and most of us (yes, even us introverts) began to crave human interaction. For me, the first 'socially distanced' coffee with a friend in her garden was something to savour; something precious regained. There were plenty of refills as we lingered, drinking in every nuance of expression as avidly as we sipped our coffee.

Let us not be too hasty to refill our diaries.

Lord, your loving-kindness leads us to repentance. Let us be those who demonstrate unusual kindness that welcomes and embraces people and brings them to your table.

Take Time to Ponder

1. Why is hospitality so important? What does it look like in your context? Is this still strong (often in tight-knit or rural communities) or has it been lost?

2. In our encounters with people, how are they made to feel? Are they welcomed, respected, esteemed or do they feel rejected, condemned, awkward or uncomfortable? Can we walk in their shoes? Can we fully enter into the experience of those who need help or does our 'kindness' make people feel embarrassed or obligated?

3. What is the motivation for giving or receiving hospitality? Are there strings attached to our generosity?

4. Are we willing to humble ourselves to receive? Do we allow people the blessing of giving to us?

5. How are we showing hospitality to the least of these, to the outcast or stranger? How do we acknowledge that the cup of water or the widow's mite is more powerful than the ostentatious entertainment (Simon's feast in Luke 7)?

CHAPTER SIX

Learning

"Take my yoke upon you and learn of me..." Matthew 11:29

Three months into lockdown, we queued in the rain to enter a shop. Two metres apart, shoppers slowly and patiently inched forward. There was no argument, no fuss; just a resigned compliance born of shared understanding.

Finally, at a nod from a shop assistant, we stepped inside. Even then, there was the ritual of hand sanitising and disinfecting the handle of our shopping basket before we could begin to choose our items.

Navigating a store became slightly comical; an unchoreographed dance routine, which involved stepping back to allow someone to pass, choosing empty aisles and quickening steps to avoid family groups. We greeted friends with a rueful smile, conscious of blocking too much space if we lingered for a chat. And there were muttered apologies when people came too close.

How did we learn all of this? In the space of a few weeks, our behaviour altered radically. We expected to stand on yellow floor markers as we waited at the checkout. We adjusted our distance, almost without thinking, as we met friends on the street. And we hurried to wash our hands when we arrived home from a trip.

We are creatures of habit. And while some of us enjoy change and find energy and inspiration in new experiences and challenges, we still have the tendency to gravitate to the familiar. Why do I always tend to sit on the left-hand side of any bus? Why do my eyes scan for the same favoured items on a menu? What keeps me coming back to old books, reading and re-reading words that are as familiar as my go-to comfort foods?

It takes powerful motivators to teach people a whole new way of doing things, especially in a short space of time. In the case of a global pandemic, there are two of the most powerful: fear and love. Whether through self-preservation or concern for loved ones, most people have chosen willingly to submit to rules and restrictions.

Here in Ireland we have an additional incentive. Our culture places high value on family and relationships, especially in the more rural areas. We have a sense of corporate as well as individual responsibility. One of the most common phrases we heard during lockdown was, "I do not want to be responsible for killing someone else's grandma."

But what has that got to do with mission in contemporary Ireland?

If our mission is motivated by a sense of duty or obligation, there is little incentive to learn and change. If mission is merely something we do, an activity, event or programme, then as long as we can tick the box, we will be satisfied, even if that activity fails to bear lasting fruit.

Incarnational mission is different. This is about the whole of life and it is focused and contextualised in a particular location or sphere of influence. It is the gospel of Jesus Christ embodied and lived out among a particular group of people. And in this type of ministry, the most powerful motivation is love. Paul talks about being "compelled" by Christ's love.[1] And if love is our motivation, we will be willing to change, to adapt and to grow in response to the changes in our environment and the needs of our people.

So a group of refugees arrived in Tullamore and William Hayes and his congregation responded in love and welcome.

So Marian Edwards and Emma Bolster Rodrigues were not able to use the Big Blue Bus during the pandemic but instead they found new ways to connect and engage with people in Ballina, going for walks or drawing words and pictures on the pavement in chalk and sharing teas and coffees with people (while physically distant, of course).

So the Loaves and Fishes Café in Arklow was shut but Robert Holden and his team stepped up to feed needy and vulnerable people throughout the lockdown.

We always begin with the one constant, unchanging truth - Jesus Christ. Everything else is subject to change. Jesus frequently described the kingdom of God in organic terms - things like seeds, plants and yeast. This is not static or stagnant. The kingdom of God is growing, developing and changing. And that brings us to our final principle: learning.

At the age of 13, my grandfather's life was transformed when an angler, fishing on the banks of the River Eden in the north of England told him about Jesus. The change was immediate and lasting. A lifetime later, I can remember him sitting in his study, surrounded by his collection of Bibles, radiant with his love for God and his passion to teach others. He owned over 30 different translations and paraphrases including a Greek New Testament that he had taught himself to read by learning New Testament Greek. He had read and reread, studied and shared God's word for years but even into his 80s, he would smile and say, "I am still wearing L-plates."

How about us? Are we willing to keep on learning and growing and adapting to the ever-changing realities that we face all around us? Or are we weighed down and unable to move?

Learning As We Go

In chapter three, we talked about 'tailgating the God of mission' - following so closely behind Jesus that we move when He moves, stop when He stops and turn when He turns. Jesus' picture of the yoke has similar connotations. When two oxen are yoked together they walk in step with one another, sharing the load.

I stumbled across an article describing how farmers in America would clear land ready for sowing crops.

> For ploughing new ground, oxen are preferable to horses. They are steadier and stronger. Formerly in breaking new land, it was a common occurrence to see several yoke of oxen attached to one strong plough; and they did yeoman service. Now in this age of hurry and rush, the slow, plodding ox has been forced to give way to the faster horse and when new ground is to be ploughed unfortunately the ox is seldom at hand.[2]

This is an important picture of patient hard work in partnership with the Lord of the Harvest, especially in the context of 'breaking new ground' - pioneering ministry. When oxen are yoked together, it is in order to accomplish a task (they would not wear the yoke in the stall). They walk and work together. And this combined, steady strength is needed to break up the soil.

We often quote these verses to people who are weary and burdened, especially with the rules and requirements of religion. But the rest for our souls Jesus offers is not simply about putting our feet up or taking a holiday. It is a new way of living that brings freedom, and it is in the context of ministry. Jesus calls us to work side by side with Him. This is about moving forward, steadily, patiently and sometimes slowly but always moving. And significantly it is also about learning. Jesus calls us to "learn of me, for I am gentle and humble of heart."[3] Although everything around us is changing, His steadfast, faithful presence is with us always, even to the end of the age.

And His presence with us is in the context of mission. We are called to "go," to be dispersed throughout the world. We have a job to do and that is not done behind closed doors. The Great Commission is not an injunction for a select few super saints, who sail across oceans and hack through jungles.[4] This is a command for every believer. Here the verb "to go" is in the present continuous tense. More accurately, Jesus is saying, "As you are going into all the world, make disciples of all nations..."

The parable of the Good Samaritan illuminates this for us. A man is attacked, robbed and left for dead at the side of the road. The priest and the Levite were more concerned about their religious duties than about the wellbeing of the man. In modern terms, they might be the 'professional' Christians - the clergy, religious orders, pastors or missionaries. Surely they would be best qualified to respond? But they walked past.

Were they too busy? Too stressed? Too preoccupied? Too prejudiced? Or did their own spiritual needs take precedence over the needs of the man ("I want to be able to enjoy my worship and if I touch this person, I will become unclean")? We all heard echoes of such an attitude during lockdown when some felt their right to worship in a building was more important than compliance with the health advice.

In contrast to the religious leaders, the Samaritan was not the obvious choice. To the Jewish mind at least, he was a foreigner and a heretic. And yet, as soon as he saw the man, he responded. His compassionate action was costly in terms of time, energy and money. This is an example of what Jesus talks about when He says we will know a tree by its fruit.[5] Even if the Samaritan did not have all the right answers, his response reflected what was in his heart.

He did not set out that morning to help someone, nor did he engineer the opportunity. He was going about his business, doing what he normally did. This was an 'as you are going' kind of encounter.

In previous chapters, we have mentioned several of these kinds of 'chance' meetings, those God-ordained opportunities that seem to fall in our laps. The question is not whether they will happen - they will - but rather, how we will respond when they do occur. The danger is that, like the religious leaders in Jesus' story, we will walk past and miss what is right in front of our eyes.

Sharing Your Lunch During Covid-19 - Ringsend

When lockdown came in Ringsend, Joe Donnelly thought he would have eight weeks to 'chill' but the exact opposite was the case. "Our local police leaders pleaded with me to keep our 'Share your lunch' programme going for as long as possible. While we had to close the café to the public, we began creating takeaway lunches for people in the community who were cocooning or self-isolating. With huge support from the community, we were able to expand the service to serve dozens of elderly and vulnerable people. Within weeks, we were delivering 150 lunches (a massive increase on the 40 loyalty cards a month provided by 'Share your lunch')."

In fact, Joe, Sharon and their team of local volunteers were able to change course and provide over 5,000 lunches during the pandemic. Talk about loaves and fishes.

Joe describes it using the metaphor of a soldier on duty. "A soldier must be willing to be re-deployed at any moment. Imagine the soldier saying, 'Oh, but I like it here. I do not want to go.' They would be court martialed. So when something like Covid-19 hits, we need to go back to our commanding officer and find out what He wants us to do. We need to be ready to be redeployed at any moment."

Learning to Travel Light

On Andrew's birthday, our daughter persuaded us to go out for a couple of hours and while we were away, she deep-cleaned the entire house, clearing away the accumulated clutter (and dust) of lockdown. What a joy and relief to arrive home and see sparklingly clean worktops and tidy hallways, to smell pine disinfectant and wax polish, and to relax in the lounge without seeing stacks of paper- these had been carefully and neatly hidden behind the sofa so we could enjoy a birthday celebration free from the stressful reminders of work.

Among the gardening, fence painting and spring-cleaning that took place in many households, the pandemic has been an opportunity for people of faith to get back to basics and do a bit of spiritual housecleaning, either personally or as a church. When all our usual habits and traditions are set aside; when our meetings, conferences and events are cancelled, it is a wonderful opportunity to re-evaluate our priorities.

Decluttering our schedules can bring relief to families under pressure and individuals who have been run ragged by the conflicting demands of work, ministry and family life. It is also a chance to ask, "Why do we do this?"

To use another analogy, when someone is pruning a fruit tree, they will cut off some dead branches but they may also cut off healthy branches in order to make the tree more fruitful. An emergency stop gives us a unique opportunity to ask those tough questions.

The danger after a sudden change is that we rush too quickly to get back to normal or we fill the gap with something else. Are we able to move forward without the clutter? Are we willing to prune even the good branches in order to bear more fruit?

The writer to the Hebrews uses the example of an athlete running a race. She will throw off everything that hinders her progress, anything that is likely to hold her back. Nowadays even the clothing athletes wear is designed aerodynamically to reduce wind resistance.

This stripping back also includes getting rid of the "sin that so easily entangles."[6] Can we allow God to search our hearts and attitudes, our long-held traditions and practices to see whether there is anything in us that is offensive?

It is all-too-easy to point out the fault lines in other cultures and the way that churches in other places have taken on board the sinful actions of their surroundings, but what about here in Ireland? Past hurts and abuses have left a devastating legacy within churches. Relationships between churches and individuals have been broken. And systemic issues of injustice, sectarianism and division have compounded the harm. Can we humble ourselves to hear what the Holy Spirit is saying to us, even when it is a painful message?

So what is left when so much is stripped away? What really matters?

I can vividly remember a moment of brokenness on a bus journey home as I prayed for my community. Feeling desperately weak and inadequate I cried out, "These people deserve better than us. We are not good enough." The answer was a gentle whisper, "Jesus is enough."

The postures of incarnational mission that we have described can enable us to respond quickly, sensitively and effectively when needs arise or when we encounter someone on the side of the road. We can change direction because we are not weighed down or restricted.

Jesus gave clear instructions to His disciples as He sent them out, "As you go proclaim this message: 'The kingdom of heaven has come near.' Heal the sick, raise the dead, cleanse those who have leprosy, drive out demons. Freely you have received; freely give. Do not get any gold or silver or copper to take with you in your belts—no bag for the journey or extra shirt or sandals or a staff..."[7]

It is interesting that here we have a similar concept to the Great Commission. Jesus says, "As you go..."[8] The disciples began to move in obedience and discovered that opportunities opened up for them along the way. They were to preach and demonstrate that the kingdom of heaven had arrived on earth but they were to do this in simplicity and weakness, without any additional resources, dependent on the hospitality and generosity of others.

We have learnt the hard way to pack light whenever we are travelling to avoid having to haul heavy suitcases through airports or on buses and trains.

Are we carrying extra baggage in ministry? Is anything weighing us down or holding us back? How can we live "freely and lightly" as we go with Jesus?

By instructing His disciples to go in weakness rather than strength,

Jesus teaches another important principle. They would soon discover whether or not they were truly welcome in any place because they were to be dependent on others' hospitality. They were to look for the 'person of peace' - someone who welcomed them in and opened the door for their ministry.

This attitude adjusted the power dynamic. The disciples were not arriving as those who were superior. There was no place for ego because they had nothing to offer except Jesus. We see this posture in Jesus Himself who did not need to grasp or hold onto position or power, but instead emptied Himself.[9]

Paul gives warnings against people who peddle the word of God for profit or those who use ministry as a way to abuse and manipulate others.[10]

Travelling light will also mean learning to cope with the inevitable disappointments and rejections we encounter along the way. When Jesus sends out His disciples in Matthew 10, He prepared them for what they will face. This is not a rose-tinted, sugar-coated ideal. The aroma of Christ will bring life to those who accept and embrace it. But to others, it will be like the scent of death.

Jesus' advice if anyone proves unworthy is, "...let your peace return to you. If anyone will not welcome you or listen to your words, leave that home or town and shake the dust off your feet."[11]

This may seem a little harsh but, in effect, He is saying, do not let rejection stick to you or weigh you down. When we allow hurts and disappointments to linger, they can destroy our peace and distract us from those who are genuinely seeking God.

I will be honest: I do not find this easy. When people reject the One who sent me, the rejection feels extremely personal. Recently, some controversy blew up over a project we have been involved in. Even the possibility of conflict left me anxious and distressed. My thought life was dominated by 'what ifs' and preparing imagined responses. I would find temporary relief in times of prayer but my mind would quickly head back to worst-case scenarios. And yet on four separate occasions, God intervened on our behalf and disaster was averted.

Like the disciples, let us allow the Holy Spirit to guard our hearts and our minds with His peace, even in the face of rejection, and learn to move on. But I may need friends to remind me of this at times and that is where travelling on this journey together can be so helpful.

Marian and Emma have encountered "people of peace" in Ballina. Here Emma shares about one of those encounters.

• • •

A Person of Peace

Ballina

By Emma Bolster Rodrigues

We were on the lookout for the gatekeepers in the town. This is a person who invites us into their home and connects us with the local community. Biblical examples include Lydia in Philippi (Acts 16), Cornelius (Acts 10) and the Samaritan woman at the well (John 4).

We met Dee in 2016. She lives in social housing in a mixed estate of Traveller and settled people. Over the years, she had been running a youth club but eventually stopped because of a lack of funding. Although not a Traveller herself, she was well respected by the Traveller community.

It was obvious that she had a huge heart for the local young people and worried about them. When we said we wanted to help, she was excited. We began organising weekly football games on a green area.

A few years previously, the local Methodist Church had invited OM Ireland's Big Red Bus to the estate to run a programme for the local children and young people. This visit left a lasting impact and Dee said the children had good memories of that time.

It was through Dee that we connected with families and with the local housing association. The estate has a community building, but it was not accessible in the evenings or at weekends. We were allowed to use it once a month and were able to build a connection with the housing officer.

Dee was curious about God and the Bible. But although she had grown up in the Catholic Church, she had not attended mass for many years and felt angry towards the church.

Then Dee had a stroke and things changed for her. It was months before she was out of hospital and back at home. Her illness caused her to wake up and start searching for God in a serious way. This time she was keen to learn about God. She felt He had given her a second chance and it was like a light switch came on. We started a Bible study with her and a few ladies from the different churches in Ballina. She has grown in her faith through that study and believes God healed her of her stroke.

• • •

Learning New Ways

New circumstances require new ways of doing things. While we all knew that in theory before Covid-19, we all experienced the practical implications during lockdown and after things began to re-open. Jesus said, "... no one pours new wine into old wineskins. Otherwise, the new wine will burst the skins; the wine will run out and the wineskins will be ruined."[12]

In a VOX magazine survey, we found that between March and June 2020, 73% of churches had organised a gathering for prayer and fellowship on Zoom, 68% had uploaded pre-recorded videos to online platforms such as Facebook, YouTube, Vimeo or to a church website and one in four posted regular devotional videos. And as churches adapted to worshipping in new ways, many also discovered new opportunities to reach and minister beyond the walls of their church buildings.

Churches of all denominations and styles have reported more people 'attending' online services or watching videos than would normally visit church on a Sunday. And some parishes have been able to engage or re-engage with people on the fringes of their congregation.

The 2020 Finding Faith Tour[13] provided stories of how churches and individual Christians not only adapted to new ways of worship but also made the most of the new mission opportunities, from online Alpha courses to delivering soup and bread lunches to the elderly and vulnerable.

In Monaghan, Rev Stephen McNie found it was relatively easy to live stream services on Facebook and YouTube, and he was delighted that over 90% of his congregation could log in to the live stream or watch the services afterwards. "We have been seeing local people engaging with us," Stephen said. "A local community group shared our links encouraging people to watch the services. One man reached out to me over the phone and prayed to become a Christian. He has a church connection but never came to that point of following Jesus. He has now contacted his pastor and his fellow church members to share the news. I have also deepened a great relationship with the local priest who watched our services."

One member of Stephen's congregation recognised the potential for reaching out to his work colleagues. He sent around the link to the live stream and invited them to tune in (a sort of "taste-and-see what I do on a Sunday morning" approach). All five of the men watched at least one of the services and two of them continued to join every week. This opened up meaningful conversations in the workplace.

In Portlaoise, Pastor Noel Cammack began going for walks in the area around his home. One day, he sensed the Lord saying, "Why don't you go on walks with me?" This new understanding changed an enjoyable outing into a spiritual act and made Noel more alert to the possibilities and opportunities all around him.

"One of the trails near our house is right next to the motorway. When I go walking, my mind is often occupied and I can be looking down at my feet," Noel said. "But on one occasion, I looked up and there was a butterfly flying. Away from the traffic, on the other side of the path, I saw all these flowers that I had never seen before. It reminded me that it is so easy to get caught up in all the 'traffic' and the busyness of life. Yet with all the complexity and the chaos going on, people have been recognising their need for God.

"On another occasion, I met a guy and when he found out I was a minister he said, 'God must sure be mad at us because of this pandemic.' I was able to tell him, 'We are living in a broken world but everything I know about Jesus tells me that He is a good and loving God.' I had a great conversation with this guy and quoted PJ Booth, 'God is not mad at you, He is mad about you.'"

These examples are not earth shattering but that is the point. Sometimes it is in the simplicity of everyday life, in the ordinary activities of work and walking, that we discover God's fingerprints. These are outside of the old wineskins of our traditions, our buildings and our programmes, but these new opportunities can provide the container for new wine.

Are we listening to the prompting of the Holy Spirit as we walk with Jesus to our workplace or to the local shop? Are we ready to find fresh ways to minister the "new wine" of God's kingdom by adapting to new circumstances and opportunities?

The exciting and scary thing about God is that He is always doing new things and His ways are definitely not our ways. In recent months, different people in different parts of Ireland mentioned the same verse from

Isaiah 43:19 (that's usually a sign that God wants to get our attention). "See, I am doing a new thing. Now it springs up; do you not perceive it? I am making a way in the wilderness and streams in the wasteland."

Creative people will inevitably adapt to circumstances and find new ways to meet a need, even with limited resources. In my early childhood, my parents were missionaries in Nepal with the Leprosy Mission. They were happy years but we lived simply and at times money ran short. That did not stop us from finding plenty of fun ways to occupy our time.

One memorable Christmas morning, a mix up occurred. Somehow my stocking ended up at the end of my brother's bed and vice versa. There was some puzzlement when my brother began to unwrap small gifts more suited to a little girl. But he showed remarkable ingenuity. He figured that the hairgrips must be some kind of new (or low budget) Meccano set, so he promptly began to turn them into an aeroplane and was a little taken aback when the mistake was discovered.

So what do we do when confronted with less-than-perfect circumstances or limited resources? Will we experience five loaves and two fish feeding 5,000 people or allow a hairclip to become an aeroplane?

Our God is infinitely creative and we are made in His image. So why do we sometimes settle for doing the same things over and over again? There is a danger, as we saw in chapter four (listening), that we seek the one-size-fits-all solution of ready-made projects and programmes rather than being willing to respond and innovate within our own context. There are some brilliant tools available that can help us as we seek to make the kingdom of God visible in our communities. But we need to be wise and discerning.

This is where it is important to embrace and encourage artists, creatives and entrepreneurs within the church community who will be able to dream, imagine and innovate new ideas. To be fair, we artists can be uncomfortable and awkward people to have around because we often approach the world in a different way. Every member of our family is a professional artist - I am a writer, Andrew and our youngest daughter are painters and our oldest daughter is an actor/singer/dancer - so it makes for an interesting dynamic. Artists and creatives bring colour and life but can also create some degree of unease or conflict, especially when people feel more comfortable with the status quo.

Yet art so often speaks the language of the heart and translates spiritual truth into sounds, images and words that resonate with our lived experience. Artists are more likely to take risks. Trying and failing is at the heart of innovation and design. I have a yearning for beauty and excellence, but I also appreciate the vulnerability of imperfection.

It was fun to watch some of the earliest attempts at video making during the first weeks of lockdown. Even if you did not set fire to yourself, there were plenty of mistakes on display and that was surprisingly endearing. We can laugh at the bloopers and quirky camera angles because they are real, raw and vulnerable. They speak to the heart of who we are as followers of Jesus. I hope William Hayes will forgive me for this, but one of my favourites is the video church service when he welcomed those who were 'also' watching online and suddenly realised that everyone was watching online.

A lot of people have become extremely competent in a short space of time as we have all learnt new skills, ordered better equipment or enrolled the help of experts. But is it wrong to confess that sometimes, the less polished early attempts appealed to me more than the competent creations of recent days?

Learning to Stretch the Boundaries

All this sounds exciting until Jesus asks us to go somewhere we do not want to go. *Missio Dei* tells us that God is already at work in the world, but sometimes we are not comfortable with what He is doing. Consider Peter and Cornelius for a moment - you can read the whole story in Acts 10. For a devout Jew, even one who followed Jesus, the idea that a Gentile could be acceptable to God was unthinkable.

Stretching the boundaries to include Samaritans was hard enough. It had not even crossed Peter's mind that a Gentile would be welcomed into the family of God without first converting to Judaism. So when Peter has a vision of "unclean animals" and a voice tells him to get up and eat, he replies, "Surely not, Lord I have never eaten anything impure or unclean." In his vision, the voice tells him, "Do not call anything impure that God has made clean." The vision happened three times and each time Peter answered the same way, "Surely not Lord."[14]

When messengers from Cornelius arrived at the house by the sea in

Joppa, Peter was still wondering about the meaning of the vision. The Holy Spirit told him, "Do not hesitate to go with these men, for I have sent them."[15] In obedience, Peter sets out on the journey, but he was yet to learn the lesson Jesus was trying to teach him. Even after walking with Jesus for three years, Peter's understanding of God's mission was still too small.

Influenced by tradition, culture and prejudice, he had set boundaries on God's grace. Somehow he had missed the memo - the recurring theme throughout the Jewish scriptures that God's chosen people were called to be a blessing to the nations, and a light to the Gentiles.

But at Cornelius' house, where a large crowd had gathered to hear the good news about Jesus, Peter was confronted with the truth when the Holy Spirit came on all those who were listening, even before he had finished speaking. This was *Missio Dei* in action. God was at work and Peter could no longer say, "Surely not Lord."

I wonder, what is our, "Surely not"? Where have we drawn the lines? Who is excluded from our comfort circle?

Recently, I interviewed Ian Dickson, the former principal of Belfast Bible College, about how we welcome and include those with intellectual disabilities. Ian said, "I remember a Church of Ireland pastor sharing a story. A family had asked for their loved one to be buried in the church graveyard but they were told, 'Because you are not parishioners, we cannot bury you within the boundary.' Eventually the person was buried outside the fence but when the family returned at a later date, they discovered the church had moved the fence. Their loved one's grave was now included. As we encounter diversity, we are going to have to move the fence," Ian explained. "We will need to expand our theological box beyond what we currently understand. Yet too often churches are unwilling to do so."

Are we willing for Jesus to lead us into new spaces that are beyond our current understanding? Or will we deny what God is doing, even when it brings life into unexpected places and among unexpected people?

Embracing Learning

I began by quoting Jesus' metaphor of a yoke of oxen. To be fair, most of us cannot really relate to the agricultural imagery of Bible times. These days, our farmers hitch a plough to a tractor, not a team, and automated farm machinery is a far cry from traditional farming methods.

Perhaps the picture of L-plates is more accessible. Even if it was several decades ago, most of us can still remember learning to drive. The driving instructor would sit in the passenger seat to guide and direct the learner through jerky starts, grinding gears and stalled engines. And in my case, there were plenty of those.

We grow in confidence but still find comfort and encouragement from somebody who sits beside us, and who has access to override controls if things get out of hand.

Holy Spirit, you lead us into all truth. Inspire us and teach us to respond to the ever-changing needs around us.

Take Time to Ponder

1. Can you remember key moments of illumination or revelation when you have understood something new about God or about mission? What brought about that learning experience?

2. Are you still wearing L-Plates? Do you cling to what is familiar or are you receptive to new things? What is the danger of always embracing 'new and shiny' initiatives?

3. Are you travelling light? Are there dead branches that need to be cut off? Do some good branches need to be pruned in order to make you more fruitful? How do we discern what is vital to keep and what should be set aside?

4. Do we serve the structures or do the structures serve God's mission? We will need a variety of structures and the flexibility to adapt to different contexts. Are you able to adapt to different situations and contexts? As God accommodates Himself to us, how easily are we able to respond to differing needs?

5. Is there any area where you are resisting what God is doing because it does not fit into your understanding? Are you willing to allow God to stretch the boundaries? Can you acknowledge that God is at work in unexpected places without feeling threatened or defensive?

CHAPTER SEVEN

Gloriously Ordinary

"... to show that this all-surpassing power is from God and not from us."
2 Corinthians 4:7

Dotted over hillsides and draped across roadside banks, these prickly shrubs have many names, from the Latin *ulex europaeus* and the Irish *aiteann* to the colloquial *whin* (especially in Donegal). They are a familiar sight if you drive anywhere in rural Ireland. The common gorse bush has lined our fields and hedgerows for centuries. But in springtime, this spiny evergreen comes into its own, set ablaze with golden flowers fragrant with the distinctive scent of coconut and vanilla.

This glorious Irish native reminds me of the story of Moses in the wilderness when he is intrigued by a strange bush (possibly a bramble) that appeared to be on fire, but did not burn up.[1] If such a bush were in Ireland, it might be accused of 'taking notions.' But this was not its own doing. The ordinary, unremarkable shrub was transformed by the living presence of the extraordinary God.

Why is this so important as we approach mission in contemporary Ireland?

First and foremost, to be gloriously ordinary is to be like Jesus. There was nothing in His physical appearance to make Him especially attractive.[2] He was a Galilean *tektōn* - a craftsman or labourer from an obscure backwater of Israel during the Roman occupation.[3] And yet this ordinary Palestinian Jew was extra-ordinary in His birth, His teaching, His miracles, His transfiguration, His death and His resurrection.

For us, Jesus embodies the six principles we have shared - demonstrating that the kingdom of heaven is so radically different to the kingdoms of this world. We see Him leaving heaven's glory to draw near and respond in compassion to those He encounters (presence).[4] We see Him, the righteous One, showing love and forgiveness to the outcasts and the 'sinners' (mercy).[5] We see Him relinquishing His rights and humbling Himself in obedience to the Father, even to the point of death (humility).[6] We see Him demonstrating respect and offering the dignity of choice instead of dictating (listening).[7] We see Him opening His arms to welcome and embrace the little children, the hungry, the strangers, the poor, the broken-hearted and the sick (hospitality).[8] We see His complete dependence on the Father ("I tell you the truth, the Son can do nothing by Himself; He can do only what He sees His Father doing..."[9]) and His gentleness in teaching others (learning).[10]

God is still on a mission, but He chooses to work through us, His body. It is His mission, *Missio Dei*. He takes the lead and shows us the way. Tailgating the God of mission (imitating Christ) seems reason enough to embrace these principles in mission anywhere in the world. And yet, as we have reflected on our unique context here in Ireland, it seems to us they have special resonance here. Consider for a moment how our land has been shaped and influenced by our history, the fault lines emerging from centuries of occupation and injustice, poverty and famine, tribalism, division and hatred, oppressive religious systems and corrupt institutions.

Addressing Fault Lines

These principles and postures demonstrate the opposite spirit. Instead of absentee landlords who profit from a distance while the most vulnerable are evicted (and it is as easy to cite contemporary examples as historical references), we draw near and become present, weeping with those who weep and rejoicing with those who rejoice. Just as Jesus became one of us and dwelt among us, so we seek to share our whole lives, to know and be known and to participate fully- in our community, neighbourhood, workplace or within a particular demographic- as we live out the kingdom of God where we are.

An incarnational approach acknowledges our limitations and weaknesses but allows the Holy Spirit to transform these into opportunities for missional engagement. At its heart, this principle is about building relationship and it is costly. Embracing presence may mean we will have to re-evaluate our priorities and our use of time, choosing people over programmes. On an island where relationship is valued so highly, where who you know is more important than what you know, this principle of presence is so vital for individuals and for churches alike.

It raises fundamental questions about our ecclesiology, especially in a season when gathered worship services have been curtailed. Can we look for ways in which God is opening new doors as we are 'scattered' into homes, neighbourhoods and workplaces? Embracing the limitations of incarnation may open our eyes to the powerful potential of the small, the weak and the seemingly insignificant.

And as we become agents of transformation (like yeast in the dough), can we come in the opposite spirit to the legacy of judgmentalism and hypocrisy of the past and the self-righteousness of cruel condemnation? Instead of the harsh, unequal judgement that singles out the poor, the outsider and the vulnerable (unmarried mothers or illegitimate children), we show mercy, just as He is merciful. Life-giving ministry will not demand outward conformity to a set of rules. Instead we seek to create safe spaces in which people can encounter Jesus. We need to invite the Holy Spirit to work, acknowledging our own brokenness as we walk alongside people in the lifelong process of healing, forgiveness and transformation (following Jesus and becoming more like Him). When we embrace mercy, we will continually re-focus attention onto Jesus, the source of life.

The wonderful truth is that as we humble ourselves to follow the God of mission, He leads us into the places and spaces where He is already at work. We come in humility, letting go of the power and control of Christendom that has at times characterised many different denominations and streams within the church in Ireland. We acknowledge that it is not about our strategies or our agendas. It is about hanging onto His coattails. Our primary focus and dependence is on Jesus. He is the 'glorious' to our ordinary and that will be evident to those around us. Our message becomes, "Join me as I follow Him. He knows the way. He is the way."

There is a stripped back simplicity to this posture that flies in the face of church growth manuals and success-oriented programmes, yet as we have all discovered, it is so often the pathway to unimagined opportunities because this "all surpassing power is from God and not from us."[11]

Embracing humility will mean relinquishing control. And in the place of surrender, He invites us to listen carefully and deeply to the heart cries of people around us, to walk in their shoes and to understand what has shaped their lives. Instead of demanding or dictating, we join the Father in this loving activity and allow His Spirit to prompt us to respond with compassion. If we do not know the question, how can we give an answer?

Responding to the needs and heart cries of people we meet will inevitably feature hospitality - a gracious, welcoming spirit that gives with an open hand but is also willing to receive. Hospitality creates safe spaces for ministry and enables us to serve the love of Jesus on a plate. This is not about courting favour or showing off to the "in" crowd but instead demonstrates "unusual kindness" to outcasts and strangers and treats the "least of these" as VIPs.[12]

Even though hospitality is deeply rooted in Irish culture, we see evidence of how this value has been eroded by fault lines of sectarianism (especially in Northern Ireland and border counties) and by racism, such as protests against refugee resettlement in places like Oughterard and Rooskey. Coming in the opposite spirit may challenge long-held prejudices. Yet Jesus invites us to journey with Him as we are going into the world.

He goes with us whether that is simply as far as the garden gate or to the ends of the earth. And instead of a rigid, inflexible adherence to what we know, we keep moving, learning and growing. We will discover new ways and encounter situations that might shake our confidence and even stretch our boundaries, but we do so knowing that the Holy Spirit is our teacher and will lead us into all truth. The kingdom of God is never stagnant and walking with Jesus, we begin to see its transforming impact on every part of life and every sphere of influence.

Mission and the Church

The focus here has been (intentionally) on mission, but that does not negate the central and vital role of the church. We began by quoting

Samuel Escobar, "The church exists for mission..."[13] If the central work of the (gathered) church is to equip the saints for works of service, then the result will be Jesus-followers who are continually sent out (scattered) as agents of transformation in everyday life.

The pandemic reminded us that the church is not a building, but the people of God. Some churches discovered the importance of 'households of faith' and of small, flexible neighbourhood gatherings. Others found powerful opportunities to minister using online platforms. Empowered by His Spirit, our calling remains to be a light to the people and a blessing to the nations. But we need to acknowledge that this is not always the case here in Ireland.

At times, the church has been affected by the fault lines of our past. Some of the issues we have mentioned such as distance, division and separation (rather than presence), or judgmentalism and arrogance (rather than mercy and humility) have hindered our witness. Especially in times of challenge, change and crisis, it is tempting to retreat back into old paradigms and remain safe within the comfort zone of our own denominations and traditions. To look inwards, to re-group and to care for our own is natural, but it can sacrifice the glorious adventure of faith waiting beyond the walls.

However, there are huge questions to explore if we are truly to embrace a mission-focused ecclesiology, which are way beyond the remit of this book. We set out to share our learning rather than present definitive or prescriptive answers. Our hope is to raise questions, encourage reflection and inspire ongoing conversation about what these principles of mission (and others we have not mentioned) might mean for the church in Ireland.

Word and Deed

Mention should also be made of the recurring debate over 'word and deed' although it would be impossible to do justice to the depth and nuance of the debate in the space of a few short sentences. Here we have simply shared our own stories and learned from an incarnational approach in Ireland. We understand the vital importance of proclaiming Christ, of demonstrating the love of the Father in action and acknowledging our dependence on the Holy Spirit's power; an integration of both word and deed. We are not presenting this as the only approach but rather sharing from our experience.

It is evident from the stories, however, that in many situations opportunities to tell people about the reason for the hope that we have come as a result of faithful, loving service.[14] So often people have been blinded to the light of the gospel that displays the glory of Christ.[15] Many seem deaf to multiple attempts at proclamation (ministry has felt like sowing seeds on a car park). But Jesus has prepared good works for us to do that have softened hearts and prompted those wonderful 'lightning bolt' moments that Joe Donnelly describes.[16]

Fruitful and Flourishing?

Does embracing incarnational mission mean our ministries will be fruitful and our churches will flourish? Not always. As every context varies, so does the fruit. Some of my co-authors have experienced exciting church growth; others are still waiting and praying for breakthrough. There have been success stories, lives changed and stories of God's supernatural intervention, but there have also been setbacks and discouragements along the way. We remain convinced, however, that as we tailgate the God of mission, we will bear much fruit at the right time if we do not give up.[17]

This road may be well travelled for some. Others may feel overwhelmed or even discouraged, wondering how or where to begin. Let us keep our eyes fixed on Jesus and as we follow Him, remember that ultimately it is God's Mission (not ours) and it is only when we abide in Him that we are able to bear fruit.

As followers of Jesus on this beautiful island, we are choosing to embrace principles of mission that enable us to draw near and to speak the good news in a language our contemporary culture can understand. We want to adopt a Christ-like posture that does not elevate us as superior super saints or impressive institutions, but rather sets us apart as blazing gorse bushes.

This treasure is in jars of clay. We are gloriously ordinary. How about you?

Take Time to Ponder

1. Which of the six principles spoke to you personally? How will you respond?

2. Which is most relevant in your church / ministry context? What other principles might be important for your church?

3. How can we continue the conversation about mission in contemporary Ireland? What other issues need to be addressed?

"Now to Him who is able to do immeasurably more than all we ask or imagine, according to His power that is at work within us, to Him be glory in the church and in Christ Jesus throughout all generations, for ever and ever! Amen." -Ephesians 2:20-21

ENDNOTES

Introduction

1 www.irishtimes.com/life-and-style/food-and-drink/even-better-than-sliced-bread-sourdough-for-beginners-1.2768363
2 Kreider and Kreider, *Worship and Mission After Christendom,* p44
3 Chris Wright *Mission of God,* p47
4 Romans 8:19-21
5 2 Corinthians 5:18
6 Genesis 12:3
7 John 20:21
8 2 Corinthians 5:19
9 Samuel Escobar, *The New Global Mission: The Gospel from Everywhere to Everyone,* p25-26
10 Ibid, p12
11 Kreider and Kreider, *Worship and Mission After Christendom,* p54
12 Stephen Neill, *Creative Tension,* p81
13 Chris Wright *Five Marks of Mission: making God's mission ours*
14 2 Corinthians 4:7

Chapter One

1 "Home to Donegal" by Daniel O'Donnell
2 "God With Us" by Graham Kendrick, 1988
3 Hebrews 4:15
4 Matthew 1:23
5 1 Thessalonians 2:8
6 John 1:1-14
7 John 1:14
8 "Let Heaven and Earth Combine" by Charles Wesley, 1745
9 John 1: 1-14
10 St. Patrick, *Confessio* 23 (www.confessio.ie)
11 www.historyireland.com/18th-19th-century-history/edward-nangle-the-achill-island-mission
12 http://trutzhaase.eu/deprivation-index
13 Alan Hirsch, *The Forgotten Ways: Reactivating Apostolic Movements*
14 Matthew 13:33
15 Matthew 5:13-16
16 Leviticus 11:44

17 Acts 8:4
18 Dr. Ebun Joseph *(VOX magazine April 2020)*
19 John 1:14

Chapter Two

1 John 10:10
2 Ephesians 1:23
3 Genesis 4
4 2 Corinthians 3:6
5 Matthew 23:4
6 Kate Holmquist, *Our Culture of Shame 2009,* www.irishtimes.com/culture/our-culture-of-shame-1.785115
7 David Kinnaman, Quoted in *unChristian: What a new generation really thinks about Christianity*
8 VOX Magazine Issuu 28, October 2015: www.issuu.com/vox_ie/docs/issue_28_final
9 This includes extracts from an article Chloe wrote for VOX magazine in 2019.
10 Brennan Manning, *The Furious Longing of God,* p77
11 Matthew 7:1-2
12 Matthew Henry *Matthew Henry's Complete Commentary* available on www.biblegateway.com/matthew-henry
13 Genesis 18:25
14 John 16:8
15 Matthew 9:9
16 Mark 2:16
17 Exodus 34:6
18 Matthew 9:13
19 Mark 3:3-6
20 Mark 3:4
21 John 8:7
22 John 8:10

Chapter Three

1 Matthew 4:18
2 Matthew16:18
3 Matthew 28:19-20
4 Matthew 11:29
5 Philippians 2:5-8
6 Luke 4:18 quoting Isaiah 61:1
7 Matthew 25:40
8 David Bosh *Transforming Mission: Paradigm Shifts in Theology of Mission,* p390
9 Matthew 14:22-33

10 Acts 16:11-15
11 www.ireland.alpha.org
12 www.praxismovement.ie/learning-communities
13 Acts 3:1-12
14 1 Corinthians 1: 27-28

Chapter Four

1 John 4:1-30
2 Luke 24:17-20
3 Helen Locke *In Search of Wholeness* - VOX Magazine April 2018, p12
4 Steve Hollinghurst, *Mission-Shaped Evangelism,* p4
5 1 Corinthians 13:12
6 Mark 10
7 www.tearfund.ie/transforming-communities/
8 Mark 2:1-12
9 Mark 1:40-42
10 Luke 24:13-35
11 Exodus 3:7-8
12 Luke 2:46
13 Matthew 9:36
14 Steve Hollinghurst, *Mission-Shaped Evangelism,* p9
15 Alex Absalom, *The Viral Gospel: How finding your Person of Peace Accelerates Your Mission*

Chapter Five

1 Kuno Meyer (editor and translator), *The Duties of Husbandmen Ériu* 2 1905, p172
2 Kathleen Simms (quoting Stanihurst 1584), *Guesting and Feasting in Gaelic Ireland,* p95
3 1 Timothy 3:2, Titus 1:8
4 Hebrews 13:5
5 Amos Young, *Hospitality and the Other,* p131
6 Acts 28:1
7 Romans 2:4
8 Luke 10:38-42
9 Mark 9:41
10 www.newgroundireland.com
11 Luke 14:12-14
12 Matthew 25:40

Chapter Six

1 2 Corinthians 5:14
2 Franklin Williams Jr., *Clearing New Land,* 1902
3 Matthew 11:29
4 Matthew 28:19-20
5 Matthew 7:17-20
6 Hebrews 12:1
7 Matthew 10:7-10
8 Ibid
9 Philippians 2:5-8
10 2 Corinthians 2:17 and 2 Timothy 3:6
11 Matthew 10:14
12 Luke 5:37
13 www.vox.ie/001/2020/5/1/virtual-finding-faith-tour-2020
14 Acts 10:14
15 Acts 10:20

Chapter Seven

1 Exodus 3:2
2 Isaiah 53:2
3 Matthew 13:55, Mark 6:3
4 John 1:14
5 John 8:11
6 Philippians 2:6-8
7 Luke 18:40-42
8 Luke 4:18-44 and Luke 18:16
9 John 5:19
10 Matthew 11:29
11 2 Corinthians 4:7
12 Acts 28:2 and Matthew 25:45
13 Samuel Escobar, *The New Global Mission: The Gospel from Everywhere to Everyone,* p12
14 1 Peter 3:15
15 2 Corinthians 4:4
16 Ephesians 2:10
17 John 15:5 and Galatians 6:9